William T. Miller

Minneapolis, MN: 1st Edition

Copyright © 2014

Introduction

If you are picking up and reading this book this tells me a couple of things about you:

First, you want to make something happen with your life. You are dreaming of the possibility of making and releasing software for fun and profit. This is the Entrepreneur in you. Like me, you want to build something great; try something new; make some money in the process, and see just how far your ingenuity and drive can take you. You are an Entrepreneur!

Second, you have some skills and interests related to technology, computers, programming, or databases. You like technology, have some aptitude, and have some good ideas for better ways to do things. You may be self-taught, or you take what you've learned in classes or on the job, and go a little further than everybody else. You know that you could make something really cool and powerful, if you had the right tool. You are or could be a FileMaker Developer.

This book represents who I am:
1. FileMaker Developer
2. Software Entrepreneur

FileMaker has allowed me to fully express both sides of my personality: I am an Entrepreneur, and I am a Techie.

Maybe you can identify.

Like you, I've never been able to pin myself down to just one definition of who I am. Sometimes I am a big idea person who dreams dreams of what could be. But sometimes I am a detail-oriented techie who can spend hours solving a programming problem with elegant and beautiful code.

If you, like me, like to dip your toes into both worlds, this book is for you.

Throughout this book, I will be going back and forth between the two worlds of FileMaker Developer and Software Entrepreneur. I hope you enjoy the ride!

It has been a great experience for me, and I am happy to share the joys and trials of being both a Developer and an Entrepreneur, or a DeveloPreneur.

Best to you,
Dr. William T. Miller II
Minneapolis, MN, USA

HighPowerData.com   SermonBase.com

FileMaker-Products.com   Spiritual-Gifts-Test.com

HighPowerResources.com

SECTION ONE:
GETTING STARTED WITH A
GREAT PRODUCT

Chapter One - What is FileMaker?

FileMaker Fact: FileMaker is a great option for DeveloPreneurs.

Easy Apps

The name of this book is "Easy Apps!" for a reason. FileMaker makes it incredibly easy for anyone to create and sell software products. Rest assured that you do not need to learn any complicated languages like Java, or C++, in order to create products with FileMaker. With its easy click and drag interface, anyone can create useful and fun applications with FileMaker.

This book assumes some prior knowledge and ability with FileMaker. You will see that as we get deeper into the sections on designing your application with FileMaker. But if you are new to FileMaker and are curious about whether this software may work for you and your interests, here is a brief introduction to this amazing software platform.

Introduction to FileMaker

Filemaker is one of the most popular cross-platform graphical database programs. It is used by millions of people and businesses all around the world. It is popular with large and small businesses; corporations as

FileMaker.

well as not-for-profits, churches, mom and pop businesses, hobbyists, and organizations of every size.

FileMaker is a database program. That means it specializes in tracking and managing information. It is not a program which someone would use to make a game, necessarily, (although it has been used for that). It is not like Java and certainly not like a C++.

It is an easy-to-use graphically-based program which allows you to create beautiful layouts using predesigned templates or your own customized layouts. These layouts can be filled with various fields for data. The data can be text, numbers, pictures, movies, sound, music, PDF's and documents files of all types.

If you are unfamiliar with FileMaker, go to www.FileMaker.com (http://www.FileMaker.com) and download a free trial version of "FileMaker Pro".

Here is what PC Magazine had to say about this release of FileMaker:

"Simply the Best"

"FileMaker reigns supreme when it comes to building beautiful, custom apps for non-programmers. The commitment to detail and

aesthetics is apparent in using the software and I actually find it an enjoyable platform on which to create an app. FileMaker Pro 13 is an easy four and a half out of five stars and an Editors' Choice for business software, and database apps."

If you are unfamiliar with FileMaker, here are a few more details you may like to know:

GUI

FM is a Graphical User Interface (GUI) application. Applications can be created with a user-friendly point-and-click system.

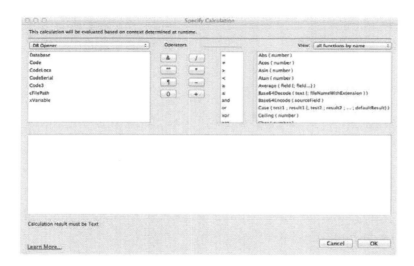

FileMaker vs. SQL

If you have heard of SQL, and think that is what a database is like, think again! FileMaker is a fun, intuitive, graphical database design platform.

Cross-Platform

FileMaker is a cross-platform software application. It is available for both Macs and PC's so that you can create products which can be used by anyone. In fact, if you release a web-based solution from FileMaker, your potential customers will only need a web browser.

RAD

FileMaker is know as a rapid application development tool. You can create amazing solutions very quickly when compared to the typical programming language.

Profitability

FileMaker, Inc. (a subsidiary of Apple) has had decades worth of profitable sales quarters, with no sign of slowing down. In fact, with the popularity of the iPhone and iPad, and the release of FileMaker GO, interest in FileMaker has never been higher. FileMaker GO has been downloaded over 1,000,000 times since its release only a few months ago. This is good news for anyone who wants to market and sell products made with FileMaker.

FileMaker is for creatives

FileMaker appeals to people who want to go out there and make something that works and looks great. Whether you are a hobbyist or an entrepreneur FileMaker is for you.

V12 & V13 layout changes

FM12 version introduced awesome layout and graphics features which amped up the already easy to use design features. Now, even people like me with no aesthetic design sense, can create great looking interfaces. FM13 has continued this trend. It now sports CSS integration which bodes well for the future design plans of FileMaker.

FileMaker is for not-for-profits

FileMaker is a great option for not-for-profits like churches or community organizations, FileMaker is a low-cost and easy-to-use alternative. With a little study anyone in your organization can become the FileMaker guru who keeps track of your organization's important data.

Connectivity Options

FileMaker has amazing connectivity options so that you can distribute your FileMaker product in many ways: mobile, using FileMaker Go, for iPhone and iPad; Web-based using FileMaker's web publishing tools; or, stand-alone "runtimes" (as FileMaker calls them). Or, you can deploy it using FileMaker Server, which allows you to host it and make it accessible over a wide area. FileMaker has additional connectivity abilities for highly sophisticated database options like SQL, along with ODBC/JDBC connectivity.

Runtimes

FileMaker has a special option to create a "runtime". This runtime program allows you to create a stand-alone version of your software so that anyone can use it, without needing to purchase FileMaker. So you can package your product into a runtime application, and sell it for a price that makes sense for your market.

There are a lot of ways to market FileMaker applications as products, such as using FileMaker Go, for the iPad or iPhone, a runtime, a web-based solution, or a standard FileMaker file which is either sold individually or hosted by a server for access by people around the world. I am a personal fan of runtimes, but there are many options which you could use to sell your product. This book will help you to understand all of your options.

Summary

Let's put this all together now. Here is how Wikipedia describes FileMaker:

"FileMaker Pro is a cross-platform relational database application from FileMaker, Inc, formerly Claris, a subsidiary of Apple Inc. It integrates a database engine with a GUI-based interface, allowing users to modify the database by dragging new elements into layouts, screens, or forms."

That's a good summary, but you need to try FileMaker to discover just how fun and easy it is to work with.

I recently had a conversation on Technet, FileMaker's on-line community for developers, with a 60+ year old FileMaker hobbyist. He said that for years he had been using a different database application. He discovered FileMaker, and said to me, "I wish I had found FileMaker years ago."

Well congratulations, reader! Because you have found FileMaker right now, and you can start using it to change your life!

FileMaker for Entrepreneurs

I interviewed dozens of people for this book. They use FileMaker every day to make a living. Some of them have designed their own FileMaker applications which they sell all over the country, and in many cases, all over the world. Others are full-time FileMaker developers who make great products for others.

The most frequent comment which I heard from them all about FileMaker is that it is a great Rapid Application Development (RAD) tool. It is great for proto-typing.

As John Sindelar of SeedCode says,
"There is no greater tool out there for prototyping than FileMaker. If you need to quickly develop a product for your first round of seed funding, FileMaker is your tool."

Right now I want to address the entrepreneurs out there. Maybe you already run your own company, or maybe you are dreaming of starting your own software company. FileMaker is a great tool to have in your tool belt. There are people who have built their entire company around one great FileMaker product.

You will meet many examples in the pages of this book. But for now, let me introduce you to to Marty Pellicore of Jupiter Creative. He and his company have made a wonderful FileMaker app for the funeral industry. It is called "Mourning Memories" and it is an application used by owners of funeral homes. It allows grieving family and friends to enter in stories and fond memories of the deceased. These stories are assembled into a beautiful printed book which is then delivered to the families as a remembrance.

Marty and his company use a number of great FileMaker features to create this product. The application itself is a FileMaker "runtime" app, and as such is a stand-alone application which does not need an extra copy of FileMaker license to run it. It is run in "kiosk mode", which is a variation of an FileMaker runtime, and mounted into a beautiful oak cabinet which is on display in the lobby of funeral home.

Jupiter Creative prepares the box, the FileMaker runtime, and then delivers a win-win solution using the data entered by the visiting families. First, the family of the loved one receive a beautiful printed book of memories. Second, the owners of the funeral homes receive the names, addresses, and email of everyone who enters information into the kiosk. This information is then available to them for marketing and business growth purposes in the future. And for Marty and his company, it is a win because he sells the kiosk solution and charges a per usage fee for the app when it is used.

Everybody benefits from this creative and thoughtful application made with FileMaker.

Dan Miller of BizTank, a business development company gave some great advice for anyone who is thinking of becoming a software entrepreneur. He said:

"You are risking everything to be an entrepreneur, so you need to get a whole lot of personal satisfaction out of the business."

FileMaker is one of those applications which can give you a great sense of personal satisfaction and fulfillment as an entrepreneur.

Products for FileMaker Developers

Now I want to address those who are FileMaker developers and want to begin releasing products in a vertical market. The advice from successful developers to beginning developers looking to release products in the vertical market is that there is a lot to do on the way to becoming a software company.

Patricia Lurvey, who sells a FileMaker product for pharmacists, shared her experience of releasing a product. She had to deal with Trademark issues, logo, tagline, license agreement, marketing, websites, support, etc.. She wisely hired a business attorney to write up the business agreement which the pharmacists would sign when they purchase her software.

Here is list of some of the actions she had to take:
"Actions taken:
- *Trademark "very fun :(process" - it was contested and that is not a cheap process;*
- *TM on logo, name, and tag line.*
- *Business attorney who wrote up the License Agreement;*
- *Also, the agreement which the Pharmacists uses to have their Clients sign, to allow them to order refills and renewals, etc. "*

I say all this not to discourage anyone, but to let you know that this book will help you address some of these hurdles.

As a FileMaker DeveloPreneur, I will help you to overcome these hurdles.

EasyApps

Chapter Two - FileMaker and HighPower

FileMaker Fact: The ease and speed of FileMaker development can help you to launch a great business.

Here is how the ease and use of FileMaker helped me start my business.

The FileMaker Developer Side of my Story:

The name of my companies are HighPower Resources and HighPower Data Solutions. One is a part-time not-for-profit business to help churches, and the other is a full-time FileMaker shop providing customized software to businesses. I'll share with you how FileMaker has allowed me to tap into both sides of my passions: an entrepreneurial vision and a technicians love of programming.

I discovered FileMaker in the mid-nineties. At the time I was a pastor and needed a way to keep track of all of my sermons. I had many drawers filled on multiple file cabinets and things were definitely getting out of hand! I couldn't decide whether to file my sermons by the date I taught them, or by the topic, or by the Bible reference, or by some other method. I didn't know what to do. I knew that I needed to be able to find them by any of those three methods. That's when I realized that a database was the answer to my problems.

So I did a little research and I discovered FileMaker. The moment I started playing around with it, I fell in love with it. It was visual, and easy, and I could very rapidly put together a tool to help do what I needed to do. Just as I said in chapter one, it was GUI, it was RAD, and it was easy!

Filemaker 4.1

FM 4.1, which I started with, was lacking in a lot of ways. But no more so than most of the other software at the time. It did what I needed it to do, so I started working with it. FileMaker, Inc continued to put out more versions and improving it all the time. And with every new version, I made my personal application to track my sermons more powerful.

FileMaker 5.5 & SermonBase

By the time FileMaker 5.5 was released, I knew SermonBase was something that other pastors could use. That is when I discovered this 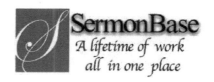 great feature of FileMaker know as "runtimes".

I loved FileMaker, because I did not have to learn a complicated software program to share my creation with other pastors. In fact, using the runtime feature of

FileMaker, I could share my creation with other pastors. With a FileMaker runtime, I could sell it very inexpensively, so that I could share my beautiful "baby" with as many pastors as possible. Churches are not known for having a lot of money for IT expenses, plus most pastors would never be able to figure out how to use a typical DB program like Access. So I made my program easy to use, and by using categories which they were already familiar with and called it "SermonBase". Since the mid-nineties, I have sold it to hundreds of pastors all over the country who want to organize and track their sermons with ease.

FileMaker 6 & MagicBase

At about the same time, my twin brother, who is a professional magician was using FileMaker to track his shows, appointments and customers. Since he knew that I was getting pretty good with FileMaker, he asked me to help him out with his application. He realized very quickly that other entertainers, such as clowns, jugglers, professional speakers, etc. needed to track their appointments, and all of the related shows, routines, tricks, jokes and  paraphernalia associated with their businesses. They also need to send out contracts, proposals, thank you's and referrals. It was a monumental task, but it was made much easier with FileMaker.

So we put together a product which we could sell to entertainers, using the FileMaker runtime feature. We called it "MagicBase Integrated Marketing Software". It did everything needed to run an entertainer's business. It tracked customers, shows, events, routines. When the customer calls, an entertainer using MagicBase would enter all the info about when, where, who, how many, how much, etc. As soon as the phone call was over, with one click of the mouse, MB would generate the customized Contract, Show Plan, Referral letter, Thank You, and the label for the envelope. It saved many hours of tedious administrative time.

MagicBase was made using FileMaker, version 6. Then, when FileMaker came out with FM7, and a dramatically streamlined file system, we redesigned MagicBase from the ground up, and released MagicBase Pro. And we sold hundreds of copies to entertainers all over the United States and in ten countries around the world. Why? Because FileMaker was so easy to use to create professional software applications!

What I have learned about creating great applications with FileMaker and building a software company, I want to pass on to you.

FM7 & MagicBase Pro & the Upgrade Process

A Lesson on Upgrading

When FileMaker upgraded from FM6 to FM7, they changed the file format. This was a great and positive change, but also presented a challenge to us. The FM7 file format and all of its features were so great that we wanted to implement them into the next version of MagicBase as soon as possible.

The biggest change was that it was now possible under FM7 to have multiple tables per file. In FM6 every table had to have its own file. Now with the new version of FileMaker it was possible to put an entire solution on just one file.

We rewrote MagicBase from the ground up to take advantage of the new features in FM7.

But once we had a new version of MB, we also had to figure out how to help our customers upgrade from the old version to the new. So we went on a long journey of discovery of how to migrate data from one solution to another one.

I share the things which we have learned, and which other developers have shared as well about the wonderful world of upgrades in Step 6 on Upgrading your Product.

ShepherdCare

After we had been selling SermonBase and MagicBase for a few years, I received a call from a pastor in Texas who wanted me to create an application for him which would let him keep track of his small groups in his church. He had a large and growing church, and things were getting unwieldy. But a database software application designed with FileMaker provided just what he needed. I called it *ShepherdCare*, and began selling that as well.

By this time, I had created my own website called "HighPower Resources" where I could market and sell my FileMaker runtime solutions to churches around the world.

FamilyFaces

During this time I had moved into the administrative side of church life, and started serving at a church in southern MN which was trying to create their own internal photo directory using Microsoft Word. This was a church of 700 people on a Sunday morning. And this photo directory was filled with photos. In fact, many of the photos were taken with cameras which were sporting many mega-pixels of resolution at this time. Thus the photos were huge! Not just in physical size, but in data size as well. Many photos were over a gigabyte. And the poor secretary who had been tasked by her pastor to make this gargantuan document, was having a hard time. It would take forever for the document to open, because of the photos, and then if she wanted to scroll down the document to access the information about some family who's last name put them in the middle of the alphabet, it would freeze up with each scroll. She would have to scroll, and then wait 30 seconds for the screen to refresh, and then she would scroll again. It was an unwieldy slow, and cumbersome data disaster!

When I was hired by the church, it didn't take me long to realize that here was another problem which FileMaker could solve. In a few months, I had built another runtime program, this time to help churches solve the problem of do-it-yourself directories. Many of them were tired of the expense and time and effort it took to hire in a big company to come in and do their entire churches' photos for the photo directly. So FileMaker and I came up with a solution. I called it "*FamilyFaces*". It was church directory software made easy.

FileMaker Certification

FileMaker Developer Tip: Get Certified!

By this point, I knew I was serious about FileMaker, so I studied for and passed the FM10 certification test. This test was required by FileMaker, Inc. to establish a certain level of proficiency for people who were either consulting or developing products using the FileMaker software. I studied and prepared for, and passed the test on my first try, and it has helped me to produced better quality FileMaker software, whether runtimes, mobile apps, or customer software. Since then, I have continued to get certified with every version of FileMaker.

If you are serious about developing software with FileMaker then you will want to pursue certification. Certification tells the world that you have a good knowledge of FileMaker and can be trusted to handle another company's data.

Go to the FileMaker.com website to learn more about it.

MinistryMaster

The most recent product released by HighPower Resources is "*MinistryMaster*" software. Like all my others, it is niche software for churches. This particular product helps churches to keep track of all of their volunteers who are serving in the various ministries and programs around the church.

TeamTracker

I have a daughter and son-in-law who are planning to serve as missionaries in another country. As part of this process they have to raise up financial support from a team of donors who will assist them with this task. This means that a missionary needs to keep track of information about hundreds of supporters. Not just information like their addresses, phone and email; but also information like, do they provide financial support? How much? How often? Have we contacted them recently? What is their preferred method of contact, etc.

As you can imagine, a missionary wants to be out doing what a missionary does, and not spending a lot of time with administrative details. So, as a labor of love for my daughter, Karissa, I created a new FileMaker runtime app

which she and her husband Matt could use. It is called *"TeamTracker"*, and it helps them to do all of the above, and then some. It has made their life easier, and they have been

sharing it with their friends at missionary school, who all want a copy also. This product is still in beta, but it looks like it is being well-received.

The Software Entrepreneur Side of the Story

When you make the decision to market your software application, you immediately move from the position of being just a developer to being an entrepreneur. In fact, in the words of Michael Gerber of the "E-Myth Revisited", you take on three roles:

You are already the "technician", that is, a person who can do a task in this case, developer software.

But the second role which you take on is the role of 'entrepreneur'. You are now not just in charge of an application. Now you are in charge of a company. You will need to run the business, track the finances, hire employees, and engage in marketing.

The third role you need to take on is the role of salesperson. If you want your application to sell you will need to take on the responsibility to make that happen. This is especially true in the early days when it is just you. But even later on when you hire a salesperson, as the owner and the head of your company, you never lose the title of 'first salesperson'. If you don't believe in your product, then your salespersons never will. So you must be a salesperson

So these are the three roles which you take on when you make the decision to sell your product:

1. Developer
2. Entrepreneur
3. Salesperson

I will show you how other companies have done it, so that you can emulate their success and build a winning company.

The Decision to Start Selling

Developing the solutions was the fun and easy part for me. But there is another side of being a developreneur, and that is the entrepreneur side of things.

I asked Patricia Lurvey, of Lyndon Consulting in Chicago, what would help her as a software business owner. She said, "My enthusiasm for my business and product got me into things that I didn't know about. Especially if you are an independent developer, there are a lot of different jobs to be done when you start selling software."

Once I had developed my various products, then I needed to figure out a way to share it with the world. I already mentioned that I had developed a website, but there was more required than just that. I had to learn how to market, how to get Google AdWords, how to develop my email list, how to send out monthly e-mail broadcasts, how to get an online commerce store up and running, and set up the merchant accounts with the bank, and become an LLC, and apply for trademarks, and track finances, and provide customer support, etc.

We will cover much of this in Section Four on Extending Your Business.

Just know that if you want to be a 'developreneur' and not just a developer, you will need to learn these skills also.

Chapter Three - DeveloPreneur Step #1 - Create your Product

Four Keys to Building a Money-Making Product

If you want to make an application which will make you some money, there are four keys which absolutely must be a part of your software solution.

Key #1 - Solve a Problem

In the FileMaker world, they are called "Solutions" because they solve a problem.

As you develop your product, the very first question you need to ask is "What problem am I trying to solve?"

In many cases, you know exactly what it is because you are using FileMaker to help you accomplish something already. You know exactly what the problem is, because it is your problem, and you are hoping FileMaker can help you solve it.

In other cases, you may not be clear on what the problem is that you are trying to solve. Maybe you are an entrepreneur who wants to start his or her own software company. In this case you are looking for a product to create. So you need to look around at your industry areas, and talk to people and find out what are their needs. For example, What is an area that is taking up way too much time to accomplish? If something is harder than it needs to be, then this is a clue to you about what your product solution should be.

For example, one client who I helped was in an industry where he needed to fill out very detailed proposals. In these proposals he had to constantly cut and paste from his company's product catalogue and specifications to various pages on his proposal, which would often be ten pages in length. He hated doing proposals because they were so tedious, and yet, proposals were how he made new customers, and made more money. So HighPower Data helped him to create a rapid proposal tool, so that the work which used to take him an hour or more, could now be done in sixty seconds! That is a problem that needed solving, and FileMaker helped make that happen.

What is most important is that you understand the needs of your industry well. Here is what Michael A. Cusumano had to say about knowing your market in his great book, "The Business of Software":

"Because software is a technology with almost unlimited applications, entrepreneurs need to acquire a deep understanding of a particular end market in order to know what to build and how to sell it."

Chris Moyer, The Moyer Group, had some similar advice:

"Start with a project in mind; something useful for you, first, so that you know what needs to be done. If it is near and dear to your heart, you should do it. Eat your own dog food, and by that I mean use your own product and see where the rough spots are."

Marc LaRochelle, Productive Computing, San Diego provided the following advice to entrepreneurs:

"Build an application that you yourself either need or are intimately familiar with. Make something practical and useable that you have a personal interest in."

Decision Point: What problem are you trying to solve?

You will want to find a very specific problem to solve. Kirk Bowman, of Mighty Data, in Allen, TX has made the observation that those in the FileMaker community who have been successful in product sales have had highly specialized products.

For example, here is a product which solves a very specific problem in the field of sports recruiting. It was developed by Paul Costanzo, of Recruiting Pro in Madison, WI:

EasyApps

Paul was a sports coach for 17 years, and he was also the Apple rep on his local college campus. So he started building a system in FileMaker to help with his own school's recruiting. What Paul found out was that there really wasn't anything like this in the marketplace. His first big client for his newly developed "Recruiting Pro Software" was Clem Haskins for the MN Gophers.

Now Paul provides one of the premier products for sports recruiting, all built in FileMaker. Paul is the classic illustration of solving a problem to begin selling your first product.

What problem are you trying to solve?

Answer this question in detail. What are the pain points which your application will solve? In your particular industry, what do you most hear people complain about? What is a problem that everyone just seems to think is status quo? That is, people just consider it to be 'part of the job' or 'that's just the way it works in our industry', etc. This is a clue to you of a particular pain point which you can solve.

When Apple developed their iPhone, the typical mobile phone hardware and software were pretty atrocious. The phones menu's were hard to navigate, and it was difficult to access key features. But everybody took it for granted until Apple came along and developed a new interface.

In your particular industry, it is the same. There are certain problems which exist right now which you can solve.

Mark Lemm, of LemmTech in San Francisco says, *"You have to find a niche that is under-served that needs some level of customization to solve their particular business challenges."*

"There is still nothing as accessible or approachable as FileMaker out there."

So the first Decision Point is this: What problem are you trying to solve?

Key #2 - Build for Revenue

The second key to building a Money-Making Product is to Build for Revenue.

What do I mean by this? Doesn't everybody want to sell their product and make money from it? Yes, but as you create your product, you need to ask yourself how else you might make money with this product besides just selling the application, which is a "one and your done" business model. The problem with "one and your done" is that when the sale is made, then you have to go out and find another customer who will buy your product. And it is hard and expensive to locate customers. So once you find one, you want to keep them as a paying customer for as long as you can. So ask yourself what are some other income streams which can be developed through this product?

For example:
1. You could customize the product if asked
2. You could sell it as a subscription for a monthly fee.
3. You could sell additional 'add-on' modules to your product
4. You could sell ads right within your FileMaker product.

Let me explain this last one:

FileMaker comes with a built-in web-viewer object. You can point this web viewer to an advertising web page. This web page would feature people in your industry field who want to sell additional products, add-ons, services, etc. to the people who will be buying your software. So you approach these third parties and sell "ad space" on your website. Then every time they open up your FileMaker product, they can see other companies who are providing services for them.

Now how you do this is important. You don't want to sell a product that contains ads. From a marketing perspective this would not be desirable. But here is how we did it with *MagicBase Integrated Marketing Software*. One of the screens in this software kept track of the magicians supplies; things like balloons, silks, tricks, cards, coins, etc.

When they needed to replenish some of these supplies, they would need to contact a magic dealer and order more. We made it very easy for them to do this by providing a web viewer on the supply page for magic dealers who could sell them supplies. Then we sold the advertising space to those dealers. It was a win for everybody.

In DeveloPreneur Step #2, Choose Your Business Model, I will share with you six different business models for you to consider as you build for your revenue stream.

You will need to think about all of these options during the product creation stage, so that you can build it now, and then sell it later, and increase your revenue streams. This also means that you will need to choose your business model as you get started. And that is the focus of chapter five. So we will cover all aspects of laying a foundation for revenue in Section Two: Laying a Foundation for Revenue.

Decision Point: How will you make money with your product?

Here is a software reality: "Distribution impacts income."

For example, the reality is that you cannot sell an App on the Apple AppStore for as much money as you can an outright FileMaker application. People are not prepared to pay several hundred dollars for mobile apps, (if they are only mobile) whereas, it is quite common to sell FileMaker apps for several hundred or several thousand dollars.

Allen Imbarratto of KiBiz has this to say:

"iOS apps have a great distribution channel, but they are nowhere near as lucrative as making a FileMaker application."

So all of these factors and more must be considered as you work through DeveloPreneur Step #1, Create Your Product.

Key #3 - Plan the Deployment

The second key to building a Money-Making Product is to Plan the Deployment

First…

Before you get too far into your project you are going to need to know what your Deployment Method will be. Your Deployment Method will impact some aspects of your design. If you plan on deploying this on mobile (iPads and iPhones), that will dramatically impact the look of your layouts. While the ultimate objective of your application may not change, the way you get there and the layouts you use to get there, will be different. Also, if you are going to deploy your product as a FileMaker runtime, then you will need to create a user interface that primarily uses on-screen buttons, as well as custom menu options. You are going to want to lock down many of the traditional FileMaker menu options .

So, **Deployment impacts Design.**

Second….

Your Deployment Model also impacts some major aspects of your business operations. For example, if you were to decide that your application must be released on a CD or DVD, and packaged in a plastic case, then that would obviously bring in a large number of other factors for your business such as production, supply, storage, shipping, returns, etc.

So, **Deployment impacts Operations.**

Third…

Your Deployment Model also impacts your things like the upgrade process. If your solution is decentralized and sitting on customer's computers and servers all over the world, then you will need an easy way to upgrade all of those applications (and preserve existing data). If you are using a centralized model, it is a little easier to upgrade, but you must still make certain that in your FileMaker solution, you preserve your customer data for the next upgrade.

So, **Deployment impacts Upgrades.**

All of these deployment decisions must be addressed before you get too far along in your product creation.

Decision Point: How will you deploy your product?

This is the third decision point for your successful FileMaker application.

Kirk Bowman, Mighty Data, Allen, TX has said that if you are in this stage, you just need to plan on making it a subscription or web-based model. Kirk has said that people in large institutions do not want to install software. They just want to turn on their computer and access what they need on the web.

But, having said that, here is another perspective on potential deployment options at this decision stage. This is from Joe Mastrianni, Happy Software.

"If it were me and I were a young fellow (which I'm not anymore), I would only do FileMaker Go solutions. Because they are easy, and they beat most of the rest out there in terms of RAD, and they are easier to penetrate the market."

When we are talking about deployment options for your product, there are various ways to do it, and not everybody agrees on the best way. Think carefully about your product, your industry, the needs and inclinations of your potential customers. Based on that, you need to make a decision about deployment which is right for you and your product.

Key #4 - Make it Work

The fourth and final key to building a money-making product, is to "Make It Work".

Before you can sell your product it must work for you, and I mean really work well. It needs to work excellently, flawlessly, and easily perform that task for which it was created.

So make FileMaker work for you. Put together a great solution. Make it functional. Make it beautiful. Not only will it be a joy for you to use as you develop your product, but it will be much easier to bring it to market.

Three Steps to Near Perfection

Here is a rule of thumb to give you an idea of the development time which will be needed for your software application to make it work really well:

1. *Borderline Functionality:* The amount of time it takes to get it 90% completed.

2. *Satisfactory Functionality*: Plan on the same amount of time to get the next 9% completed. So if it took you 200 hours to get to 90% completion, then plan on another 200 hours to really get it humming nicely.

3. *Near Perfection:* Plan on the same amount of time to get the final 1% completed. If you want near perfection, "Apple-style" level of perfection to a product, then you will need to spend the blood, sweat and tears for the final 1% by spending another 200 hours to get to that point.

Do you want to know how many hours it will take to complete your project?

Get it 90% done and then multiply the number of hours so far, by three.

Yes, it is painful.

Yes, it is tedious.

Yes, it is worth it!

However, an important part of getting that 1.0 product out the door is finishing it up. I asked Matt Navarre of

MSN Media, in Portland what a product developer needs to avoid, and he said, "Avoid feature bloat!"

"Don't spend too much money on 1.0. Let the first customers pay for 2.0.

Don't over-analyze to see if there is 'space'. If you know it is needed, just do it.

It is difficult to make an accurate prediction of if a product will be successful, even if others are there. The big question is How good is your Product, and How Good is your Service?"

Just get 1.0 out the door, and then save some features for 2.0. This is a real danger. Deb Zempel, of Deborah Zempel Consulting, shares about an experience she had with a company that was trying to commercialize a product. But they kept adding more and more features to it, and the product never made it out the door. She made sure when she started her own product company that she did not make the same mistake.

If you want to improve your product's design to near perfection, then you need to check out the "Master Class" by Albert Harum-Alvarez of SmallCo.

Here is how Albert describes it:

"MASTER CLASS - A place where you take something you've worked on and receive immediate critique from a mentor and fellow students. Four or five days of class, and you have then evolved your solution so you can see a major rethink."

The Master Class is usually provided two times a year in Miami and the Hamptons. At a recent Product Conference which I attended, I was able to participate in a mini-mini version of such an exercise. In one session, three of us were able to present our products to the seminar attendees and then to get feedback from Albert and the attendees. It was kind of a scary experience, but also really good for product functionality, design and perfection.

If you want to improve the performance of your product, you could learn by following the example of Patricia Lurvey, of Lyndon Consulting. She told me that when she developed her FileMaker application used by pharmacists, she included a software agreement which says that they will send data back to her company. The data would be sent in an aggregated, anonymous format, and would be used for improvements in the software.

The lesson is that if you plan it out ahead of time, you can improve your product's Design and Performance right from the beginning, in Version One of your product.

The point here is that you can overdo a good thing. The goal is to get the product out the door. But you want to do this by avoiding two common mistakes. The first is releasing a subpar product, and killing off future sales because of negative comments from early adopters. The second mistake is feature creep which prevents the product from ever getting out the door.

Develop your Beta-Testing Plan

Your product solution is going to have bugs.

So make sure you provide enough lead time before you take it to market, in order to test and find and fix all bugs. You need to let others try out your product beforehand.

Test, Test, Test!

Jerry Robin, Transmography, Phoenix provides FileMaker Coaching. He told me that

"you need to build a robust solution that can handle different customers and different workflows. This is a design issue. Debugging a product is critical. It must be bullet proof!"

Danny Mack of New Millennium Communications in Boulder, CO concurs with these comments:

"The difference between what they built for a small number of people vs. a commercial product; the range of ways they can break your solution is wider than you could ever imagine. They will do things you would never have thought of; they will do things in different order. You need to code 'defensively', and error-trap. Anticipate errors right from the beginning, thus making longer scripts. What would happen if an error happened here? What kind of pre-testing do you do?"

This brings up the necessity of providing a beta-testing plan for your product. Major corporations spend millions of dollars testing their solutions. But I am guessing that you need a good beta-testing plan that will get the job done without spending a lot of time or money.

How to develop a good beta-testing plan:

First, define exactly which areas need testing.
Yes the whole solution must work, but you will have a pretty good idea after developing and using your solution, where the potential problem areas are. Think about those and the types of errors which could possibly occur. Make a list of all key areas, actions, buttons, scripts etc, which you want to be sure to test out. Decide how long it will be tested, and in what way.

Second, develop a beta-testing team.
You could test the product yourself, but the best course of action is to develop a beta-testing team. When other people test your solution, they will find and do things that you never would have dreamed of, resulting in a more thoroughly tested product.

The easiest way to do this is to use your list of already interested people. This list is developed concurrently with your product. To see more details about it, see the chapter "Market Your Product", which will explain list building. Decide what you are willing to give to beta-testers.

Typically, it is a completely free and unlocked copy of your product upon release.

When I was developing my most recent release, I posted on my website that I was looking for beta-testers. I also sent an email blast to my prospects indicating the same. As a result, I received a number of interested contacts.

Third, define a beta-testing plan.

Putting together a beta-testing plan takes planning to make sure you benefit from the effort. Here are four things which I've learned while beta-testing my products.

Four Elements to a Successful Beta-Testing Plan

There are many things which you could do when beta-testing. Here are the four steps which I take for my products:

1. A Non-Disclosure Agreement (NDA)

Because you don't want them talking about your product before release, or sharing it, or worse, stealing it, you need to begin with an NDA. This tells them you are serious about protecting your intellectual property. It is not a guarantee of theft, or sloppiness, but it is a help towards the goal.

2. A "Time Bomb"

Be sure that you build a date timer into your software, so that it expires after a period of time. This is much easier to do, if you release your beta-versions as an FileMaker runtime, limiting access to the file. When the beta-test period is over, it will no longer open. Even if the final product may not be released as a runtime, this is a great way to provide some initial testing of your product at an early stage without giving everything away to somebody who might take your IP re-engineer it.

3. A Beta-Tester Response Method

Third, give them a form to complete and send back to you. This could also be a website. You can require them to complete all parts of the on-line form before being taken to the final screen which may have some sort of reward or incentive.

Here is another way of getting good response from your beta-testers: Rather than waiting until the end to complete one form, you can give them a series of response forms along the way. As they make their way through each stage of your software, you encourage and reward them, and also get immediate response and feedback for each section of your software.

For example, set up an automated response email system, so that whenever someone signed up as a beta-tester, they would a pre-determined set of emails. They were delivered in the same frequency, and asked each beta-tester to try the same areas of the software, which I had previously determined in my Testing Plan.

4. A Reward or Incentive

Thank your beta-testers when they are done, and send them a final copy of the completed product.

Summary

You want to balance and maintain two distinct goals for this Fourth Key of "Make It Work".

First you want to be able to release a great product that solves a problem, and 'wows' your users. But secondly, you don't want to take forever to get to this stage, so you need to have an effective process that allows for development, testing, and then release in a timely manner.

So those are the four keys to building a money-making product:

1. Solve a Problem
2. Build for Revenue
3. Plan the Deployment
4. Make it work

WORKSHEET:
GETTING STARTED WITH A GREAT PRODUCT

Here is a quick form to complete before you move on to the next section:

The Four Keys of a Successful Product:

Key #1. Solve a Problem - What problem are you trying to solve?

How have others tried to solve it?

How is your product unique in its approach?

Key #2. Build for Revenue - How will you make money?

What other options do you have besides just a one-time sale for a revenue stream?

Key #3. Plan for Deployment - How will you initially plan to deploy your product?

Key #4. Make it Work - How will test and perfect your product?

Who will help you with this?

Bonus Section - Why FileMaker is a Great Choice for Product Creation

In the course of my interviews for this book, I had the pleasure of speaking with many FileMaker enthusiastic developers. Below is just a sampling of a few of their comments about why FileMaker is a great choice if you want to make and sell software applications.

Allen Imbarrato, of KiBiz Systems:

"The thing that makes FileMaker the best is that it is a great proto-typing environment where you can flesh things out and get all of your features together."

Deepali Gokhale, InfoCypher Systems:

"FileMaker has a lot of advantages in terms of rapid development and ease of use. It is a great platform for mobile applications. If FileMaker, Inc, does it right I think that FileMaker is going to be around for a long time."

Jonathan Fletcher, Fletcher Consulting:

"FileMaker is absolutely in the perfect position right now with GO and iPads."

Hal Gumbert, Camp Software:

"There is no reason you can't do it. There is a great FileMaker community to help you succeed."

Marty Pellicore, Jupiter Creative:

"Not only can you build something quicker and easier with FileMaker, but it also lends itself to making a product that will get things done. ... Definitely do a runtime because then it can run on both platforms (Windows & Mac)."

Nicholaus Orr, Goya Ltd. Australia:

"Go for it. Every platform has it's strengths and weaknesses. Think about what the strengths of FileMaker are as a platform and work with them. Don't try to turn FileMaker into something it's not."

David Knight, Angel City Data, Los Angeles:

David has some great things to say about why FileMaker is a wonderful choice for designing your first software application product:

1. "FileMaker has incredible ease of use, with a great rapid application development environment. You can literally start designing right now. It allows you to capture the design ideas before you have to figure out all the engineering."

2. "FileMaker offers unparalleled prototyping".

3. "FileMaker has great fidelity on both platforms. FileMaker has done much of the heavy lifting. You don't have to define all the minutiae of how large/long to make each field, setting indexes, etc."

4. "FileMaker Server as a hosting environment is a great eco-system for your files and deployment to customers. It simply doesn't require the babysitting that many SQL applications do."

5. "The total cost of ownership is typically less on an FileMaker system. ROI as a developer is also great, as you can often program things in 200 hours vs. 2,000 hours, like in other products."

6. "Key: FileMaker makes it easier to start a product company."

Doug Rawson of BaseBuilders, Reno NV:

"Yes, absolutely use FileMaker. There are always pros and cons to any system, but FileMaker has made it simple, such that our company is not a large company with a large development team. You don't need to have a large team with FileMaker. It makes it so cost-effective to develop the product. And then to get an app that is cross-platform that would be extra hard. What other platform will let you do that?"

Vince Mennano, Beezwax, Oakland, CA:

"Why FileMaker for Product Creation?

"In general, one of the strongest points of FileMaker is that you can iterate rapidly."

"The idea of being willing to try out an idea, and then change it, or even abandon it as needed.

Because FileMaker as a tool can give you the ability to iterate rapidly and try things out and see how it works."

Mike Clements, BakeSmart, Indianapolis:

BakeSmart is a vertical product created with FileMaker which operates on a subscription model. What separates it from the competition in the bakery and ingredients field is that it includes a Customer Cake Module for bakeries which do a fair amount of custom work.

I asked Mike why he chose FileMaker to create his outstanding product:

"There are pros and cons to be sure.

Pros -

1. Development speed;

2. Immediate feedback, with no compiling or uploading, etc. to see what you've

done.

3. The integration of SQL has been a good benefit;

4. All the plugins available;

5. The 3rd party developer community of FileMaker.

Cons -

1. Much more limited pool of developers to choose from

2. Versioning is a bit of a challenge. "

John Sindelar, SeedCode, Seattle:

1. "FileMaker will help you get to revenue quicker than anything else."

2. "FileMaker mission is to let subject matter experts build their own tools.

But the ability to make an app, and the ability to make a software company are two different skills. You need more to succeed. Find your channel."

Matt Petrowsky, FileMaker Magazine:

"There are so many things which you have to do in order to come from a solution idea to a complete package, and no one can compete with FileMaker in that area."

Albert Harum-Alvarez, SmallCo, Florida:

"FileMaker is wonderful for quick iterations. It is built for that. ... FileMaker gives you quick life cycles on the product."

Don Clark, FM Pro Guru, Albuquerque, NM:

"The great thing about FileMaker is that it is a RAD platform. It is easy to make additions and changes. And it is easy to rectify something if a mistake is made."

"If you look at PHP or Java, it is a much more formidable learning curve.

And then there is a lot of compatibility issues, where they 'deprecate code' (when moving from 4 to 5), then your code just stops working, usually because of security problems."

Summary

So as you build your commercial product, FileMaker is a great choice to develop your product. As I have indicated, the primary factors which you are going to need to incorporate into your solution are:

Success Factor #1 - Solve a Real Problem
Success Factor #2 - Build for Revenue

EasyApps

Success Factor #3 - Build for your Deployment Method
Success Factor #4 - Build to Near Perfection

FileMaker can help you do this better than any other development platform out there

Bonus Section
100 Great Ideas for Knowledge Products

Introduction

Sometimes all you need is a great idea.

In the following Bonus Section are listed 100 ideas for your own Easy App. These are just the germ of an idea, to get your thinking. Each of these ideas are related to knowledge and information which would work great with a database application. Read through this list and find yours. Then get started with building your Easy App.

~~ *BUSINESS APPLICATIONS* ~~

Apartments to Rent by City
This could be a WebDirect solution which is available to anyone from the web.

Architectural Designs and Buildings
Grouped by category with beautiful photographs in container fields.

Bartender Drinks Mixer Catalog
Recipes, plus you could include videos of how to mix each drink.

Bicycle Parts
Links to vendors, manufacturers, parts shops with quick email links to order parts on standardized forms.

Books & Library DB
A lot of these have been done, but who knows, yours could be a winner!

Cars
Available for rental or sale

Car Parts

Chiropractor Office
Check-in form for patients. Have them fill out their forms on iPads and load it into the doctor's client database automatically.

Computer Store & Electronic Components

500 Great Coaching Questions for Life Coaches
Develop a collection of great questions grouped by topic and then provide an easy to use interface to quickly assemble a Coaching Session.

Crime Tracking DB by City to be sold to city governments or public awareness groups

Dating - online Dating Site

Website Domains to Buy, Sell, Rent
There is a big market for selling domains.

Customers
Just a general customers interface which could be used by many mom and pop shops.

DayCare
Pictures of the little cherubs with allergy and health instructions; permission forms; parents and guardians contact info.

Ebay Sales Tracker

Flowers & Roses
Some people love flowers. Make it easy for them to view them with beautiful pics, and order them from suppliers, wholesalers, and florists.

Goals
Create an easy to develop goals planning system.

Junkyard Business and Parts Tracker

Manufacturing Company

Medicines and Pharmaceuticals

Products Catalog

Prospects & Leads Tracker for Salespeople

Psychological Tests

Lists of all tests, grouped by category, where to get them, automatic ordering, lists of clients who have used each test.

Real Estate

Tattoos Cataloger

Easy to scroll pics of all the types of tattoos. Put it on an iPad so the customers can easily view and select them, without having to lean over the counter and look at pics hanging on the walls.

Wedding Dresses

What a great opportunity to showcase beautiful dresses.

Wiki Generator (categories, subs, and sub-subs)

This could be an all-around wiki generator for any industry. Just fill in the Categories, Topics, Subtopics, and Descriptions, and the DB assembles it all into a beautiful display and/or printout.

~ *EDUCATION* ~

Art - Renaissance Art with pics
Great opportunity to provide a study tool for students.

Biographies - Mini-Bios of Great People
Lots of people want to learn bio's but don't have time to read thick books.

Chemistry formulas

Countries of the World Atlas

Educational Tests and Measurement Tools

Elements database
There is already a beautiful app for the iPad for this, but maybe you could improve on it, or make it available thru web direct.

Flags of the World (with pics)

Flash-card Math Tester

Grades Tracker
For teachers, accessible from home or school, with links for parents

Jeopardy-like Trivia Game

Historical DB
Track great events by year, such as "This Day in 1877..."

Human Anatomy
With a section by section visual display

Language training

Lesson Planner

Literature DB
Track the great literature and provide synopses

Mathematical & Statistical Formulas

Physics forumla DB

Quotations

Scientists
Great Scientists thru History. You could do searches by topic, field, century, gender, country, etc.

Scientific Formulas and Theories

Spelling Quizzer

Make a fun game, using FM13 slide controls.

Star Systems

Wonders of the World

~ *ENTERTAINMENT* ~

Bands

For people who love their music!

Comedic Routines

This is no joke! List of routines by topic, audience, etc.

Comic Book Collectors

And for once, you can use Comic Sans freely!

Computer Games

Crossword Puzzles

Games

Strategy games DB with lists of all expansions available and collected so far.

Horse Racing Results

Deploy this for an iPad so they can take it to the track.

EasyApps

Jokes and Riddles

Manga Comics Collection

Monty Python Trivia and History
For something completely different!

Movies

Music collection
Especially for classical music collectors

Video Collection

World Records

~ *FILEMAKER* ~

FileMaker Custom Functions

FileMaker Plugins

FileMaker Reference (to Functions & Calculations)

FileMaker Certification Test Quizzer

~ *FINANCES* ~

Money

> Expenses & Accounts; watch out Quicken!

Retirement Accounts

Precious Metals

Stock and Assets DB

~ *HIGHPOWER RESOURCES* ~

Just for the fun of it, here are the databases which I provide through my two companies, HighPower Resources and HighPower Data Solutions.

Empower

Special Abilities Tester

TeamTracker

For missionaries and other workers raising support

HighPower Library

Very simple library DB

FamilyFaces

Photo Directory for organizations

ShepherdCare
Small Groups Tracking Software

HighPower Data Suite
Business software for customers, products, invoicing.

MinistryMaster
Volunteers job, skills, and gifts tracker

SermonBase
For pastors, providing a complete archive of all sermons

MagicBase Pro
For magicians, tracking shows, events, routines, customers

~ *HOBBIES* ~

Antique Collectors DB

Beer Varieties; Beer Cans with Pics; Micro-Brew Recipes
This is a big area of interest.

Bird Watchers (with pics and audio tweets!)

Car Collectors

This would have pics, statistics, history, etc.

Card Collectables (like Magic the Gathering, Star Wars)

Chess - Openings

As a former USCF ranked player, I know this is a huge area of interest here, definitely needs a database to track it.

Chess - Tournament Results

I kept my list in a notebook for years.

Coin Collection

Lego's

Yes, people like to take a pic of their creation and store it before they tear it apart.

Golf Courses

Guns & Rifles Trivia, History, and personal collection

Great Stories & Illustrations for Toastmasters & Presenters

Military Battles
Do a search by country, by year, war, General, etc.

Puzzles
Some people like to take pictures of their 1,000 piece puzzles once they are done, and then keep record of it.

Rock Collectors
This is big business for some, collecting, storing, selling.

Star Wars Collectors
This would be a geek's paradise. You can include room for storage of pics of all of the paraphernalia, actors, history, backstories. Add in a fun trivia game.

Pez Dispensers
Yep, people collect these, and you could sell them the database to track them all.

Recipes
This is a no-brainer need, and if you make a beautiful display, and interface, you could be a winner with this one.

Route 66 Discoveries

People still get their kicks on Route 66, and this could make it fun for them.

Scenic Views (of America, by State, by Country, the World)

This one could be filled with container fields for pics of America, and the world. Do search's by State, Country, site, etc.

Sources for stories

Writers keep a collection of ideas for stories, and these need to be tagged by topic, person, place, event, story-line, etc. This DB would need to have major and easy to use search capabilities built into it. It might be nice to provide a large open space for writing story snippets as well. And then add in an easy to export feature for word processors.

Spices

Their uses and applications and history and pics

Stamp Collecting

As you may know, philately is a major area of interest for many people. You could supply them with the application to make it more fun and interesting for them.

Travel - Great Travel Sites

US National Parks

~ *HOME & FAMILY* ~

Cats, Dogs, Birds
This could be a care and how-to guide for animal loves.
You could also make it easy for them to fill the DB
with cute pictures of their cats!

Family History & Genealogy
This is ripe for the use of a database to track all of the
relationships. This would bring a whole other meaning
to "relationship graph"!

Family Photo Album
Someone needs to come up with a nice replacement for
the old family album which works better than iPhoto.

~ *SPORTS* ~

Sports fan love their stats, and any of these would offer
great interest to their respective fans.

Football Stats and Facts

Baseball Stats & Facts

Olympics DB

Golf

BasketBall Stats and Facts

Horse Champions

SECTION TWO: LAYING A FOUNDATION FOR REVENUE

Chapter Four - DeveloPreneur Step #2 - Choose Your Deployment Method

Introduction

Deployment options are closely tied in to your Business Model, but they are technically distinct.

The Business Model is the system you will use to actually make money; how your Customers will pay your for your Product.

The Deployment model is how your customers will access and use your product. Some types of deployment automatically require a matching business model, but not always.

For example, Doug Rawson of BaseBuilders sells a product for architects and engineers called "Praesto AE". When the customer "purchases" the file, Doug's company installs it directly onto the customers system (server and clients). In this case, it seems like a one-time purchase option. However, he is actually using a Subscription Model. The installed files check in with the BaseBuilders main server once a month to make sure the subscription payments are up to date, and warns if not.

So it is important to consider all of your deployment options before you begin, because your method of deployment will impact your Design and Development.

You have two choices when it comes to Deployment. You can use either a Centralized or a Decentralized deployment model.

Choice #1: Centralized Options:

Centralized Options means that you only have one deployment of your application. You customers access their data through your server.

And even with Centralized Deployment, you have two other Options:

Option #1: One Application with Multiple Tenants
This is the multi-tenancy model. All of your users and their data are actually inside of the same data file. Data is kept separate through login ID's.
Multi-tenancy has potential problems, as any bug or mistake could expose all of your client's data to everyone else in the system. But it is being used by some people successfully. For example, I recently developed an app for a truckers association in Tanzania which uses the multiple tenancy model.

Option #2: Multiple Applications - Single Tenant in Each
In this version, everything is on your servers, so it is still a centralized deployment option, but you create a separate copy of the program for each customer. This is

obviously a more expensive option. It requires more server space. But the advantage is that each customer has free reign within their data and there is no chance of mixing client data.

Choice #2: Distributed Options:

In the Decentralized, or Distributed Model, your application is installed, either by you or by others, directly onto the various servers being used by your clients, around the world. The downside of the Distributed Model, is that when it is time to upgrade, you will have more difficulty than with the Centralized Model, which requires an update of only one application.

In the Distributed Model, you have perhaps hundreds of deployments, each unique in their own way in terms of hardware, access codes, transmission speeds, etc. It is a major undertaking to put together a good updater to handle all variations. But it can be done. We deal with that in the chapter on upgrading your product.

Deployment Options:

When it comes to deploying your product, FileMaker gives you a number of great options:

Six Deployment Variations

Options mean complexity. For example, Allen Imbarrato, of Ki Biz Systems has said:

"I do a lot of coaching for product developers. Now it is more complicated because you have to deploy on web, or mobile, or client app."

Not only can you deploy in a centralized or a distributed fashion, but you also need to plan for how clients will access the data, no matter where it is stored. Will they be using desktops, mobile, or web?

Deployment Method #1: Desktop Installation

So, what are your options?

1. Desktop Installation

This uses a standard .fmp12 file (open and unlocked)

In this method, you are simply selling a copy of your FileMaker designed product directly to your customers, and they are placing it on their computers. This is in harmony with the 'one and your done' business model.

The advantage of this model is that, as the sales company, you do not have to worry about installation, maintenance, and upgrades. From a commercial perspective, once they buy the software appellation from you, it is all over; the sale is complete, and it is their responsibility to install and use it.

Of course, it is not that simple, as there are usually support and upgrade issues. But this deployment option is the simplest of your available options.

Deployment Method #2: Hosted File

A hosted solution is one of the most popular in the FileMaker world. The hosting can be done either locally, from a server box sitting right on the customer's premises, or through a hosting company.

In the past, it was much more common for companies to keep their data on their premises for the hosting. The problem with this is that you have to have someone on staff who can handle all the IT problems that come with hosting your own solution. This would include, down-time, security, upgrades, internet and intranet issues, etc. If your company was too small to afford its own IT guy, then you would have to bring in a hired gun once in a while to fix problems. This also could get expensive.

This is, however, losing favor to more web-based methods and subscription models. Nearly all of FileMaker's competitors are coming from the web-based deployment model. This is both good and bad. In my interviews for this book, I spoke with many developers who were rather concerned about the prospect of FileMaker, a primarily server-client product, trying to compete in a space against many web-based products. But Marc LaRochelle, of Productive Computing in San Diego, take a much more optimistic outlook about this. He says that

Many people still favor the Client Server model because
1.   Traditional expectations

2.   Not everyone is comfortable having their data in the cloud, exposed on the web
3.   You still can't beat the speed of a local server or runtime.

So his company has turned it into an advantage

But Productive Computing also provides FileMaker hosting for those who want it and because they have multiple data centers across the country, users can get a great experience.

As Marc says,

"Because we have a team of certified developers on staff we find ourselves offering strategic partnerships with other developers making vertical market solutions."

Whichever hosting solution you go with, your deployment issues are more or less the same. You will need to get client copies onto your customer's computers, and make sure they are regularly updated and maintained so that they can make good use of your great FileMaker hosted solution.

Deployment Method #3: Mobile

When you are deploying for mobile, you will be using FileMaker Go to allow your customers to access your application on their iPads or iPhones.

In the opinion of many developers, this is the only way to go right now. Mobile computing is hot! People want to have access to their data on their iPhones and iPads. FileMaker is in a great position to take advantage of this with the release of FileMaker Go. Everybody is asking for a mobile version of their app. If you can offer your customers the ability to access their data on their mobile devices, you will be in a winning position.

At a recent FileMaker developer's conference, in the words of one session presenter,

"If you are not developing your solution to be used on a mobile device, you are developing a legacy solution."

Those are strong words, but they ring true today. The presenter has been saying this for years, but only recently has this fact caught on.

Here is a great sales pitch which is used by many developers: *"I can put your data on an iPad."* Just that simple sentence excites people, and they ask how. I have seen this in my own consulting practice. When I create a mobile solution for customers, their friends start telling them how cool it as and asking who made it for them.

And the real value, as a FileMaker developer using FileMaker Go, is that you can create and deploy a mobile solution much more quickly and cheaply than anyone else. The time frame to measure the development process of a typical iOS app, is measured in months, not weeks. (This includes the sometimes onerous process of getting your app approved for the AppStore.) But for FileMaker developers, the process of releasing an app for mobile deployment is measured in weeks, and even days in some cases. FileMaker, Inc., has already done the heavy lifting by getting FileMaker Go approved. Now, using FileMaker Go, as a shell, you can simply drop your app into it, and you are done.

The importance of Mobile Deployment:

Jonathan Fletcher, of Fletcher Data Consulting and co-host of the FileMaker Talk podcast:

"There is no easier way to get an app onto the iPad than with FileMaker."

"FileMaker is absolutely in the perfect position right now with GO and iPads."

Deployment Method #4: Runtimes

Another deployment option available to your as a FileMaker developer is a runtime. (If you are not sure what a runtime is, please see the chapter in this book about FileMaker runtimes.)

Runtimes have their advantages and disadvantages. Runtimes are great if you need to release a solution to people who do not have, or cannot afford, to use a typical FileMaker client software. Or maybe you are releasing a tightly controlled commercial product, and you want to control the menus the buttons, the authorization, the imports and exports, etc. You can take control of all of that by deploying a runtime.

Here are some examples of ways in which people have made use of runtimes:

1. Mike Larkin of MacMagic in MN has used runtimes to provide sample demo copies of his software solutions to customers. They want to see and try out some of his software so he has created a locked-down runtime version. This version will sometimes have more limited capabilities, or else, a date time in it, so that it will turn off after a certain number of days or uses. But this allows him to distribute the software to his potential customers; let them try it out; and then pay him to get the real thing.

2. Shin Nagawa of Splash Software in Japan tells of a company which needed their employees to get through a very specific process of recording and tracking some data for a limited period of time. So they created a runtime solution which they made available on the company server. Their employees downloaded the runtime and completed the process as directed by the runtime. There was great consistency across the company records because the runtime provided a strictly guided process.

3. Vince Mennano, of Beezwax, is the Director of FileMaker Development who released the awesome analysis tool called, "Inspector Pro" as a runtime. Look at the Inspector Pro runtime version as a great example of

presentation. I use it myself all the time in my work on various projects.

4. HighPower Resources, the not-for-profit arm of my company, provides runtimes to churches, because many smaller churches simply can't afford the fees necessary to purchase multiple copies of FileMaker client. By selling them runtimes, they get a great deal, and I am able to reach more churches with our data services.

Here is a powerful example of a runtime deployment:

~~ PRODUCT FOCUS: MOURNING MEMORIES ~
by Marty Pellicore of Jupiter Creations

This runtime solution is distributed in its own very fine oak cabinet and placed in the lobby of funeral homes around the country.

Here's how Marty met a need with a FileMaker product:

Marty's product helps people to write out and record memories of loved ones. Using the kiosk, people locate the name of their loved one. Then they are able to enter some loving and kind words about the deceased. These words are then gathered into a beautiful bound book for the family. As an added marketing bonus the names, and emails of those who enter their information is made available to the funeral home.

Marty explains the advantage for the funeral home with this example: "there was a funeral with 1600 people who signed the guest book. But the funeral home couldn't read 400 names and so the funeral home lost 25 % of their potential market.

But with Mourning Memories visitors enter their information directly and it is captured by Marty's ingenious program. As people sign the book, and submit it, the program sends it to his server. And if there is no internet connection, it will wait and send it when one is established.

The kiosk station uses a Mac Mini, a 17" monitor, and a keyboard installed in a nice oak case, which is then placed in the lobby of the funeral home.

In terms of the business model, customers have three financing options:
1. They can buy the kiosk unit and pay a per usage fee (for each funeral).
2. They can lease the unit for a monthly subscription and a per usage fee.
3. They can use a Pay per Use fee only.
Obviously the usage fee increases with each of these options, with the third option costing the most per usage.

That is a great example of a runtime version of FileMaker being put to good use by a smart and ingenious developer.

Deployment Method #5: Web-based

When I refer to web-based deployment options, this could include using WebDirect (FM13+) or IWP (FM12 or earlier) or CWP (all recent versions).

1. Web Direct

Since FileMaker 13, there is a great new technology available to you called, "WebDirect". WebDirect has replaced what was called Instant Web Publishing in all previous versions of FileMaker. While IWP was rather limited in its functionality, WebDirect, presents a true "FileMaker" user experience. FileMaker's ease of use, pleasing user interface, and rapid development ability can now be offered online through the web direct feature.

For those still using FM12 and earlier, IWP will work and provide a limited user experience. You will not be able to control some aspects of the visual look and feel, and there are some significant usability limitations. But it can be done, as I and many other developers have proven.

2. Custom Web Publishing

The other option which continues to be a possibility with all versions of FileMaker is Custom Web Publishing. CWP is a PHP-based framework providing much greater control over the web-based user experience. It translates the various FileMaker commands into PHP commands for use on the web page. PHP provides excellent control, but it is detailed work which requires considerable skill to implement.

3. Other Web-Services

There are other ways to make use of FileMaker on the web:

To quote Jonathan Fletcher:

"There are a massive array of API's on the internet that will work with FileMaker. For example, the web viewer in FileMaker uses the Google API.

"Another example of web services is Google Docs which has an API, so you could make a spreadsheet to talk to FileMaker.

"360Works has a WebServices plugin, so you could use an FileMaker Server to host a Web Service. Also FeedZone is a great example of a company totally focused upon providing web services through FileMaker.

"Also, RestFM by Goya, will allow you to do various operations using FileMaker data directly from the web.

"A lot of CC gateways have API's where you can create your own query and have it respond to you."

Chris Ippolite, of iSolutions, has a website dedicated to HTML5 integration with FileMaker.

Deployment Method #6: Subscription Model

Some people use the term "SAAS" or the Software As A Service model, while others use the term "Subscription". While there is some difference between them, for our purposes the Subscription model requires the customer to pay a monthly (or quarterly, or annual) fee to keep the product working.

The subscription model is becoming increasingly popular. Many major companies and services such as SalesForce, are completely subscription-based. And many FileMaker developers have found this model to be both easy to implement and financially lucrative.

In this model, people do not purchase a FileMaker file from you. They rent the software from you while it is hosted on a server. They pay a monthly subscription fee for access to the product.

The advantages of the subscription model for the customer is that it has a much lower entry point. For a low monthly fee, they can have all the advantages of a very comprehensive software system and not have to pay the thousands of dollars it would cost to buy it. The advantages for the development company is that it is much easier to anticipate and manage cash flow.

Doug Rawson, creator of Praesto AE software for architects and engineers has said that when the economy went south a few years ago, the fact that they had recurring monthly income from their subscription model is what helped keep them afloat.

This model can be tricky to implement. You will need to work with your hosting company to get the right set up. In fact, as an FileMaker Developer you have to realize that FileMaker does not make this model easy. Allen Imbarrato of KiBiz Systems says that he does not use this model because FileMaker doesn't make it too easy to use the SAAS model. The reason for this is because you can't control the filenames and IP addresses. If you have a mutli-file solution and you have to change filenames, it breaks the relationships. Sometimes one wants to dynamically control filename and IP addresses. But right now can only use one server per client.

Deepali Gohkale, Cyber Consulting says:
"There is a huge movement of SAAS on the web and FileMaker has a lot of constraints for that."

This illustrates that there are pros and cons either way. Many people swear by the subscription model. But for others, they find the implementation and security necessary to be a bit cumbersome.

How to Get Paid with a Subscription Model

Doug Rawson of BaseBuilders, Reno, NV has a very creative system for keeping the money flowing in every month.

"Within Praesto we have a date-sensitive activation code that expires every month. Then we have another solution which tracks their CC, and every month it charges them. The code lasts for 40 days, but they receive a warning before the end of the month."

"We had to do the encoding/decoding of a cryptic activation code, which included, among other things, a DateStamp, a Client Number, and the Number of Licenses. After the Activation Code downloads, then the Client system decodes it and assures that it is paid for, and applied to the correct person, and licenses."

Doug calls this "MailBox Money".

That is one way to make sure you get paid every month, by using the Subscription Model.

Summary

There are other variations of these six deployment methods, but this covers the most popular options. Most successful businesses use a combination of these deployment options depending upon the needs of your customers and the unique aspects of your product category.

These deployment options show you the great variety of choices which you have for distribution of your product to your end-users using FileMaker technology.

Consider these options before you begin to design and develop your software application.

FileMaker Developer Discussion: The Data Separation Model

In the FileMaker community there is a lot of discussion about the best method for deploying your solutions, for one key reason. FileMaker Pro, unlike many other database systems 'merges' data and user interface.

For this reason many developers advocate the "data separation model" where you deploy into two, sometimes three, files for a solution that would otherwise be contained in one file.

In the Data Separation Model, one file is used to keep all of your data, and the other is used for interface and layouts. FileMaker Pro doesn't make it easy to do this, but many people have created such a solution and loved it. Others don't care for the data separation model, because they think its an additional expense for the customer in development time which is often not worth the benefit, unless you have an extremely large and complicated solution.

I prefer to use the single file model (which was one of the truly great benefits of the .fm7 file change). Instead, I prefer to create an upgrade process which makes it easy for customers to move from an old version to a new. When we created MagicBase Integrated Marketing Software, which was used by customers all over the US and ten countries of the world, we made a "one-click" upgrade. Using the Troi File plugin, we just asked them one question, "Where is your original folder?" Once they answered that, we took care of the upgrade for them.

You will need to make the decision on data modeling before you begin development.

Chapter Five - DeveloPreneur Step #3 - Plan Your Business Model

Six Possible Revenue Streams from Your Product

Introduction

Although they are different things, your Business Model is intimately tied to your Deployment Method.

There are a number of business models which you can choose from. In this chapter, I will review six different models you could use. But what I noticed most as I interviewed software development firms is that there are a huge number of variations available to you as you develop the business model best suited for your particular industry. These have been grouped into main headings, but the variations are limited only by your own imagination.

Now that you have made some key decisions, you are ready to choose your business model:

Business Model #1 - One-time Purchase

This is the "one and your done" model. Once your customer buys the product from you, there is very little need for additional contact. They may contact you for tech support, but there is no more revenue after the initial purchase. This works and there are many out there who make a successful living with this model. But you may want to modify this model a bit.

The upside of this model is that it is easy, quick, and simple.

If your only plan is to sell the individual software applications one by one, then it will be difficult to make a substantial profit, unless you really have a hit on your hands. I've been told by the experts in this industry that those who have made the most money with a business model aimed primarily at software sales, have sold a highly specific software to a tight niche industry.

One example of someone selling a specific software to a tight niche industry is Joe Mastrianni of Happy Software, based out of New York. They sell to government housing organizations who need to track their clients. The software is called *Housing Pro,* and it satisfies a very specific niche in a specialized market.

But even in this sort of a situation, Joe recommends that any business focusing on software sales, always makes sure that they sell a service contract as part of the deal. So, while primarily using the software sales model #1, their business is not limited to it. They also sell maintenance contracts with their software. In fact, the maintenance fees are substantial enough that they can include updates and service contracts.

Here is a word of advice from Joe Mastrianni about the software sales model:

"Sell the Software but require a Service Contract on it."

In the early days of Apple's AppStore, most of the applications sold were the one-time sales purchase variety. But then as the market matured, Apple made it much easier for companies to offer "in-app purchases". This became especially useful for games, and so another revenue stream was created for developers. Perhaps as you give thought to your business model, you can plan for some way to tweak the one-time purchase model to provide for some additional revenue streams.

Business Model #2 - Customization

There is a great market for customizing FileMaker applications. A number of FileMaker companies offer "starter" solutions, which are almost completely usable applications but which can be customized for a fee.

~~ Company Focus on the Philosophy of Customization: Angel City Data ~~

The reality is that many customers will want their solutions customized to their specific needs. This provides a great income opportunity for you and your company.

As David Knight of Angel City Data has said,

"People like buying things that have been bundled together, as long as they can

make a few adjustments to it. For example, at McDonalds you may hear, 'I want the Coke with the #6 item, but no pickles.'"

How you market your customization options for customers is also important. David describes customization words like, "snap-in options", "configuration" and "tailoring". All of these are different ways of expressing what you can provide for your customers in the manner of customizations. How you explain customization is as important as what you provide.

Here are the various starter solutions provided by Angel City Data which may be customized:

Nimbus

• Full-featured Contact and Project management system

Asset Tracker

• Take full control of your digital assets

Fire Inspection Management

• Keep a full inventory of buildings and their characteristics, schedule inspections, track violations

Warehouse Management

• Inventory Tracking/Receiving/Delivery/Invoicing

Music Production Management

However, total customization may not be the way to go either. If you allow your customers to change everything, it could lead to a bit more chaos than you desire.

So Danny Mack of New Millennium Communications, Boulder handles it this way; He says,

"We allow some customization; a "hybrid-customization". They can change some things but not everything."

For some companies, customization alone is not enough: Allen Imbarrato, Ki Biz has said that they sell products which they customize, and that this was better than just doing brand new custom design work:

"For us, selling and customizing our products was a better way to go than being just a new custom design house. We have like 20-30 customization projects going on right now."

So start with a product, customize it, and make money.

Summary:

The goal for many new developers then, would be to create your own starter solution which is completely usable but also easily able to update with additional modules and customization.

John Mark Osborne, FM DataPros also an accomplished developer concurs with these comments:

"Sell the Solution (as a template) and then Customize."

"90% of projects start with a pre-made solution, that then gets customized."

Business Model #3 - Subscription

The subscription model is a wonderful option for providing on-going income.

Many customers will appreciate not having to fork out a substantial quantity of cash up front. The idea of a small monthly fee is very attractive.

I've spoken with many developers who used to use the one-time purchase model and have made a switch to a monthly subscription model. The reason is because it is better for your customers, and better for you as a developer. For example, Albert Harum-Alvarez told me that he used to sell one of his products as a one-time purchase, combined with maintenance fees. He has since rolled those into one monthly subscription fee. It works better for everybody.

The subscription model is a great example of how you need to determine your business model while you are still developing your solution. If you intend to use the subscription model there are a couple of ways you can do it. You can use either the centralized or distributed models which were discussed in the chapter on deployment.

The Reverse Authorization Process

Many people have had the frustrating situation in which a Microsoft app which they have fully paid for, warns them they are using a 'non-licensed copy' and shuts one out of his or her own application. This can be extremely frustrating and so one FileMaker developer, Hal Gumbert of Camp Software solved this problem by turning the authorization issue on its head.

The only time someone is prevented from using the app is if their name is on the 'have not paid' list; in this case, the solution shuts down. The advantage of this scenario is that all customers are allowed to continue using the solution, even if for some reason they do not have internet access. But whenever someone logs in to the solution and has access to the web, the solution checks to see if they are on the unpaid list; if so, it shuts down.

What about those who will just stay disconnected in order to save a few dollars? The reality is that if you are providing a good service for your customers, these sort of individuals will be in the minority and not really a threat to the business. Eventually they are going to go on-line and when they do, it will shut it down until they have paid.

One other revenue stream which is close to the Subscription Model is the Maintenance Model. In this model, there is typically an annual fee, called a Maintenance Fee, which must be paid by all customers. The purpose of this fee is to cover the cost of upgrades, tech support calls and emails, and basically anything necessary to successfully keep the customers solution up and running.

~~ FileMaker Product Focus ~~
Pool Pro Office by Gerard Beutler

One company decided to give customers a choice between how they would finance their product by giving them the option to choose between a Subscription Fee or Maintenance Fee. The company sells a product called "Pool Pro Office". Their pitch is that it will provide "Perfect Project Pricing" for pool construction. It is an estimating tool. It also provides a project status board, leads, pricing, and maintenance. A vertical solution using Subscription fees for access to the server, or an annual Maintenance model for stand alone clients.

This is a very successful product, and Gerard Beutler, the developer, has received the "Mad Dog Award" from FileMaker, Inc. Their product was also featured in a FileMaker promotional article. I asked Gerard why customers choose their product. He said,

> *"They choose our product because of ease of use. If you can start the internet, you can use our product."*

Pool Pro Offices gives their customers a choice, either they can access the centralized software using a Subscription Model, or they can install it on their own machine and then pay a Maintenance Fee. If they choose to subscribe, then they can also access the product using

FileMaker Go. Since the Pool Pro Office company are members of FBA, when the customer buys the product, they are automatically buying in to the most current version of FileMaker licensing as well.

Another aspect of this product is that they use SuperContainer for their large images, even though FM12 and later have improved storage capabilities for container fields:

"One of the best things which we have is the ability to store images and documents, using 360Works SuperContainer. FileMaker external container is slow to back up large images, even though they are stored externally still takes time every time you do a backup. SuperContainer actually sits on their machine and provides for a quicker backup."

For updates, they use Refresh FileMaker from Goya.

Variable Price Model

Just because you are providing a Subscription Model, does not mean you have to charge the same price of all customers.

Paul Costanzo of Recruiting Pro Software, Madison, WI has a three-tiered pricing model for his sports recruiting software: Silver, Gold, and Platinum. The beautiful thing is that all three tiers use the same codebase. Depending upon the pricing level, the application just accesses the preferences, checks their payment level and unlocks only those parts of the solution which has been paid for.

The highest tier also includes a certain number of hours of "free"customization.

Summary

So you can see that something as simple as a subscription model has a number of variations available to it.

1. Centralized Application with Remote Login

2. Decentralized Application with Remote Authentication and a Positive Authorization Scenario

3. Decentralized Application with Remote Authentication and a Negative Authorization Scenario

When you make these decisions before you build your app, you can design scripts to match your business model.

Business Model #4 - Per Usage

Another great business model is the Per Usage option. In this model, your customers don't pay anything unless they use your system. This is an easy entry option for customers who may be reticent to jump into some new software.

This is attractive to a lot of people. For example, don't you hate it that you have to pay some $60 a month cable subscription fee for dozens of channels you never watch? That's the way some people feel about their software. They may not want to pay a monthly subscription for something they only use a couple times a month. You will need to look at your audience and your industry and decide what is the best option.

FileMaker, Inc, itself has recently switched to a per usage model with their new WebDirect technology. When you access WebDirect from FileMaker Go on a mobile device (iPhone or iPad), then the FileMaker Server software tracks how many "concurrent" connections exist. If the usage surpasses the number of connections which have been licensed, then the owner is warned and will have to purchase a server license which allows for more concurrent connections. Now technically, this is not a pure 'per usage fee' in that you have to purchase a certain number of licenses for WebDirect connections when you buy FileMaker Server. But it is a per usage fee system in that if more people are using it, then you need to pay more.

Business Model #5 - Training

Another business model which still works is the Training Model. In this business model, you balance the cost of the software between the actual software sales (or subscription, customization, or usage), along with the additional cost of training. This is a situation where you require training to be included in the deal. You sell the software at maybe 75% of your value, (thus under-cutting the competition), but then you charge for monthly or quarterly training. These can be on-site or webinars. Through this additional training then you can provide your customers with better know-how in using your software. This will translate into greater customer satisfaction, and for you, it will help you to recover the additional revenue for your product. What's more, you keep and maintain a close working relationship with your customer. As an added bonus, you can offer additional product features (such as additional for-purchase modules) during the course of the training classes.

Training, however, has seen better days, according to John Mark Osborne of DataPros. While much of his company used to be based on training, the expanded opportunities of YouTube make it easy for people to find training without having to pay for it. So your business model must account for this reality.

Of course there is much to be said for live interactive training (whether on site or through a webinar). YouTube and Lynda.com videos will not compare to the many benefits of the personal interaction which live training affords.

There are a couple of variations you could do here is well. One is live onsite classes or webinars, scheduled at a particular date when everyone joins. The other is paid access to training videos. In this case you would have a large collection of training videos which you make available to those customers who buy the "Premium" version of your product.

Business Model #6 - Freemium Model

The freemium model has a long history of success for many businesses. In this model, you give something away for free, and then offer expanded product modules for a fee or premium. Many companies will offer excellent FileMaker starter solutions completely for free. One of the key requirements of a great "freemium" model is that what you give away has to have real value. It needs to be a good deal; something that people want. This also increases people's feelings of loyalty and commitment to the company that gave them such a great solution for free. This is the "free" part of the plan.

One example of this is Richard Carlton of RC Consulting. They provide a very comprehensive application called "FileMaker Starting Point". This application seems to have everything: Customers, Products, Estimates, Purchase Orders, Invoices, Inventory. But Richard has said this is a "starting point" only. They give this away for free, which is amazing because they obviously invested hundred of hours developing it. But then as Richard told me, many customers come back to them to get it customized.

The "premium" part of this solution can be approached in one of two ways:

Option #1: Unlockable Modules for a Fee

These modules are already in the solution when it is given away, and for a fee, the client is allowed to use them. Of course, you would need to be certain that the solution is free from hacking. With FileMaker for the average client you could give away the free application in an "almost unlocked" state; that is, one in which almost all menu options are available, but the person does not have the [Full Access] privilege set turned on. This would allow you to lock them out of parts of the solution that have access to Modules.

Option #2: Customization for a Fee

The second option of the Freemium model would be to give away the basic solution completely unlocked, and then offer to customize it and expand its abilities. Note that this model is slightly different from the Model #2 - Customization, in that in this model, you actually are giving away something of value to the customer. They can take your solution and use it, and never come back if they do not wish to. This is unlike model #2 Customization, where they purchase the solution from you, with the express intention that you will customize it for them for a fee.

Each has its advantages. In the Freemium model, you can always attract potential customers with the word, "free". In the Customization model, you are guaranteed additional income with a sale of the software, but you may not attract as many customers as a Freemium model may.

Protecting Your Revenue Stream

We also need to address the threats to your revenue stream. The issue of software security has to be addressed by every software entrepreneur and FileMaker developer.

The premiere expert in the FileMaker community on the topic of security is Steven Blackwell. In interviewing him, he had the following things to say about this important topic:

"1. The FileMaker products have a very good security suite. The level of security from .fp7 to .fmp12 has substantially improved. "

"2. The theft of FileMaker software products is fairly pervasive, in the following three ways:

First, those who want to steal the intellectual property and adapt it for themselves.

*Second, those who want to steal the software
and use it for their business.*

*Third, those who want to unlock it and sell it on
the black market and keep the money."*

*"3. Three Step Goal of Blackwell's security
work: Close vulnerabilities, Block the threat agent,
and Mitigate the impact."*

Your beta-testing process needs enough time to test the security of your solution thoroughly. Ask your testers to break into it in any way they can. Based on their results, you can determine appropriate steps to secure your intellectual property.

Conclusion

Each of these Business Models has their advantages and disadvantages. You will have to decide which is the right model for your particular solution.

Some can be successfully combined as well.

Choosing your business model is the fourth Decision Point which you will need to handle if you want to build a successful software company by creating and selling FileMaker applications.

Worksheet: LAYING A FOUNDATION FOR REVENUE

1. Primary Deployment Question:

Will you be deploying as a Centralized or Distributed solution?

2. Secondary Deployment Options:

Which will you choose?

Option 1 - Desktop

Option 2 - Hosted

Option 3 - Mobile

Option 4 - Runtime

Option 5 - Web

Option 6 - Subscription

3. Business Model Choices

These are related to and dependent upon Deployment, but still distinct.

Which will you choose?

Model 1 - One-time Sale

Model 2 - Customization Income

Model 3 - Subscription Income

Model 4 - Per Usage Fee

Model 5 - Training Charge

Model 6 - Freemium

Bonus Section:
Decision Points for your Product

We are part of the way through the process of planning your product. Here are the decision points we have covered, along with those we have yet to consider.

Decision Points:

1. Problem: What problem are you trying to solve?

2. Revenue Streams: How will you make money?

3. Deployment Model: How will you Deploy your Application?

4. Data Access: Will your customers access your solution through Desktop, Mobile (iPhones & iPads), Web or all three?

5. Distribution Model: Will your product be Centralized or Distributed?

6. Business Model: Which of the six models will you use?

7. Product Media: Will you be selling just digital (1's & 0's) or also media, and hardware?

8. Authorization Codes: Will you use random numbers, or link it to each customer?

Marketing: How will you let the world know about your Product?

9. Upgrading: How will you manage Updates & Upgrades?

10. Support: How will you keep your customers happy?

SECTION THREE: DEVELOPING YOUR FILEMAKER APPLICATION

Introduction

This book presumes some previous knowledge of FileMaker. This is not a book about the basics of developing in FileMaker. The goal here is to help those who know how to use FileMaker generally, but want some specific guidance on how that relates to making and releasing a software Product using FileMaker.

The next three chapters covers the specifics of product creation as it relates to runtimes, mobile products, and web products.

Chapter Six - Special Focus: Runtimes

Runtimes are a very unique aspect of the FileMaker solution. The ability to make stand-alone software applications which will run without needing FileMaker has long been a part of FileMaker. In speaking with Ryan Rosenberg, VP of Marketing and Services for FileMaker, he said that they are continuing to discuss the role of runtimes in FileMaker. It looks like it will continue to be part of the FileMaker universe, for the most recent release of FileMaker, version 13 has not only continued to include the ability to create runtimes, but they added in an additional functionality to encrypt those runtimes.

The Unique Value of Runtimes

"Runtimes" as FileMaker calls them are not for everyone. They are useful in special situations. For many companies, a traditional deployment approach such as server hosted software may be a more appropriate solution.

I happen to like runtimes. They hold a special place in my heart because it was the ability to make runtimes which first got me really hooked into using FileMaker. At the time, I was using FileMaker just for myself to track the sermons I was creating and using in my church. Then, when I realized that other pastors could be helped with this kind of tracking ability, I wanted to share it. Fortunately, I discovered that FileMaker had the ability to create a runtime so that I could share my creation with other pastors.

So, what is a "runtime"? This is the word which FileMaker uses to describe an application created with FileMaker, and then bound together with a FileMaker 'engine', so that the primary FileMaker application is no longer needed to use it. This allows a person to make and sell applications which do not require your customers to own a copy of FileMaker.

The key advantage for not-for-profits like churches is, of course, that instead of having to pay several hundred dollars just for FileMaker, and then more for the software I was making, they could get the whole thing for much much less than the cost of FileMaker. This was extremely attractive to pastors who don't have a lot of extra spending cash for software, and may not have the time to learn to use a program like FileMaker.

Primary Benefits of Runtimes

So what are the benefits of runtimes?

If these work for your particular industry needs, then you should give runtimes a consideration as a possible deployment option:

#1. Low-Cost Entry Point

They are inexpensive to sell, because the customers do not have to pay an additional money for FileMaker.

#2. Ease of Use

They are dead simple to start using. Just double-click on the icon and you are up and running. No need to install it on a server. No need to hook in through the internet. Just download it to your computer and get to work.

#3. Easy to Deploy

Usually, customers can just make the purchase on your e-commerce site; download it, and start using it immediately.

#4. Great Option for Demo's

If you want to give customs a taste of your software before they buy, a time-limited runtime is a great option.

Downsides to Runtimes

There are, however, some downsides to Runtimes:

#1. Difficult to Upgrade

You must figure out your upgrade plan before you release Version 1.0 of your software. I can't tell you how many hours I spent developing updaters for my various runtime solutions. It can be done; but it is tricky. But now with tools like "RefreshFM" by Nicholaus Orr of Goya, that process is much simplified.

#2. They are typically single user solutions

One person can use the software on one computer for each runtime.

#3. Limited Network Ability

Although there are hacks out there, runtimes are designed to not access networks, and simply be used by individual users.

If you are a developer who understands what "codesigning" an app is, and need to get it done, then contact Christian Schwarz of MonkeyBread Software in Germany. He has an app called "Codesigner" which will take care of that for your Mac OSX needs.

By the way, MonkeyBread also offers a product for runtimes called the "Runtime Shrinker" which will make your runtime files (which tend to be pretty large) much smaller.

How to Create a Runtime

FileMaker Pro vs. FileMaker Pro Advanced

You will need to purchase FileMaker Pro Advanced in order to make stand-alone products which you can sell. It cannot be done with the basic FileMaker Pro application.

Developer Utilities

You create the runtime by accessing the Developer Utilities menu item

"Developer Utilities" can be found under the "Tools" menu of FileMaker Pro Advanced.

Solution Files: Add File

When you select "Tools/Developer Utilities" you will be presented with the "Developer Utilities" screen.

In the upper right is an Add button. Click this button to bring up a browse selection dialogue box that will allow you to choose the FileMaker files which you want to add as part of your runtime solution. You only need to choose one, but you can include more than one file in your solution. Whatever files you add to your runtime solution will all receive the same "Bindkey" (to be explained later). This

Bindkey is what links them all together and lets FileMaker know they are part of the same runtime solution.

Renaming Files

Once you add the files into the "Solution Files" list, you can change their names to something that would be acceptable for a commercial product.

To do this, click once on the file name in the Solution Files list, and then it will appear in the "Rename file" dialogue box. Change its name to whatever you like and click the "Change" button. Or if you decide you do not want a file in your runtime solution, select it, and click the "Remove" button.

Primary vs. Secondary Files

The first file added to the Solution Files list will be designated as the "Primary File". This means that it will be loaded first and will be the anchor for the runtime engine file (which will be added later by FileMaker when you create the runtime). Once you've added all the files you need for your runtime solution, you may designate any of them to be the Primary File. To change the Primary File, click in the small grey margin to the left of the files and the red arrow will designate the new Primary File.

Project Folder

Once you have added the files you need to your solution, you'll need to designate a Project Folder for your runtime solution. When the runtime solution is created,

FileMaker adds a number of helper files into the root folder of your solution.

Three additional items are added into your runtime root folder besides the files which you designated as part of the runtime solution.

First, FileMaker will add an "FileMaker Acknowledgements" PDF. This indicates all the various licenses from FileMaker, Apple, and many others which are a part of the solution. You are legally required to distribute this document with your commercial runtime solution.

Second, FileMaker will add the FileMaker "engine". It will typically end in ".app" (on Macs), and will be rather large, at about 160 MB. This is a special version of the Filemaker application which is tied to just your runtime file through the Bindkey.

Third, there will be a folder called "Extensions". Inside the Extensions folder is another folder called "Dictionaries". Because FileMaker is an international product, it includes files from about 13 countries.

Checkbox to "Overwrite matching files within the Project Folder"

The Developer Utilities has a checkbox entitled, "Overwrite matching files within the Project Folder". If checked, any files with the same name will be overwritten. If it is unchecked, then FileMaker will create a new runtime folder every time you create a new runtime.

Application Code

You can apply whatever file extension you like to your Runtime. FileMaker defaults to applying the .usr or .fmpusr extension, but you can make your own.

Since I sell five different products, each of my products come with a three digit extension, the first two signifying my company name and the last, the individual software (.hps, .hpc .hpm .hpf .hpl).

You can register these extensions with Microsoft or Apple, but you don't have to.

An issue you will need to address with your extensions is that the security on the operating systems may warn your customers or even prevent them from installing it.

If your business model includes offering Demo's or Trial software and your prospects may not know or trust you in the beginning, then this warning may stop them even installing the Demo/Trial. So give that some consideration and perhaps register your software extensions.

However, Apple's new security which they installed with Mountain Lion and forward, defaults to preventing the installation of any software not purchased through the App store.

I've helped several of my customers navigate their way through the Mac system settings to disable this feature.

You may need to address this on your website when you sell your product or offer Demo files.

Solution Options

On the Developer Utilities screen there is a button entitled, "Solution Options". It opens the "Specify Solution Options" window which has five checkbox options:

1. Create runtime solution application(s)
2. Remove admin access from files permanently
3. Enable kiosk mode for non-admin accounts

4. Database must have a FileMaker file extension

5. Create error log for any processing errors

In FileMaker 13 you are presented with two additional options on the Solution Options page:

6. Enable Database Encryption (or Re-encrypt files)
7. Remove Database Encryption

Solution Option #1: Create Runtime

Create runtime solution application(s)

On this mini-window, there are a lot of additional selection options with a brief description of what it does, such as:

- Runtime name: You can enter anything you like here
- Extension: FileMaker provides a suggested extension, "FMPUR", but you can enter your own extension.
- Bindkey: FileMaker will create a timestamp in the Bindkey dialogue box. You can enter whatever Bindkey you like. If you create end up creating multiple FileMaker products, you will want to use a different Bindkey for each product.

Three other items on the page are:

- "Closing Splash Screen Preview" button - lets you see what the image will look like when the solution closes.

124

- "Custom Image" - Click the "Specify" button to choose the image you would like to display when your solution closes.
- "Delay (2-12 seconds)" - There is a small entry box where you can specify the number of seconds that the image remains on-screen.

Solution Option #2: Remove admin access

If you choose this option then you will not be able to open it up and work with it. Removing administrative access means that no one, not even FileMaker Inc will be able to open it up and access it.

When I first began releasing my products, I selected this option in the name of security. But I discovered that when my customers came to me for tech support issues, I was unable to open up their copies of the solution using my own copy of FileMaker Advanced.

So in the end, since it was making life more difficult for me and my customers, I no longer use this option. Security is provided for by other means.

Unless you have a tremendous security issue at hand, or are in real danger of significant theft of your solutions, you should keep the Admin access open. The person this will help the most is you.

Solution Option #3: Enable Kiosk mode

Here's what FileMaker has to say about kiosk mode:

"Kiosk mode is a way of displaying your database solution or your runtime database solution on a full screen, without any toolbars or menus. As the name suggests, Kiosk mode can be used to present your database to users as an information kiosk."

Kiosk mode on Runtime?

Kiosk mode is a great option for FileMaker runtime developers.

One app developer who is doing a great job with runtimes in Kiosk mode is Marty Pellicore of Jupiter Creative, who I have spoken about already.

Solution Option #4: DBs must have FileMaker extension

The fourth option on the list is "Databases must have a FileMaker file extension." With this option, all files will be given the FileMaker extension.

Solution Option #5: Create error log

The fifth Solution Option checkbox is "Create Error log for any processing errors."

This log file will list any errors which were encountered while processing the runtime. You'll also have the option to choose its location.

Solution Option #6: Enable Database Encryption (or Re-encrypt files)

FileMaker describes it this way:

"Encrypt a copy of the selected database files by entering a FileMaker account name and password that is assigned the Full Access privilege set and then assigning an encryption password. Files encrypted at the same time have the same encryption password and shared ID."

This sixth option has the following elements on the screen:

"Shared ID:" This is similar to the runtime option available for the first checkbox.

In order to use the encryption option, you will need to supply a FileMaker account which has full access. You will also have to supply an Encryption Password. Selecting this option allows you to enter a password and a password hint.

Finally, there is an option related to storing images, entitled "Keep Open Storage". With this option, your images will be accessible in the file structure and non-encrypted.

Solution Option #7: Remove Database Encryption

The seventh Solution Option is to Remove Database Encryption. In order to do this you will need to enter the identical password which was entered for option #6 to encrypt the file.

You will also need to supply an FileMaker Account which has full access authorization.

Other Options: Closing Splash Screen image

FileMaker allows you to brand your product with your own logo. This final splash screen image will appear for a few seconds when the program shuts down.

The number of seconds which it will be displayed can be selected as well. Your options are anywhere from two to 12 seconds delay before the image disappears and the file shuts down.

Load & Save runtime settings

Once you create your runtime, you may want to keep the settings so that you can re-create it again and again without having to reselect everything.

Creating a template folder

I've found that many times there are several other files, folders and documents which I want to include with my product. These could be documentation files, "ReadMe" files, or End-User License Agreements (EULAs). Many times, as I plan for updates and upgrades I pre-set additional folders named "Backups", "Updates", etc.

I keep all of these additional files and folders in a "Template File". Then once my solution is created, I simply drop them into the primary runtime folder of my product solution. Then I compress it and my product is ready to go!

Create it!

Finally, you are ready to create your royalty free FileMaker runtime solution to sell to your customers!

Click the "Create" button and let FileMaker do its work. It will take a minute or two for FileMaker to assemble the runtime creation. When it is done it will be in the solution folder which you specified.

The folder will contain all the files associated with your product, plus the FileMaker runtime engine which is fairly large. FM13 has improved runtimes such that they are smaller than those made with previous versions.

Also contained in the folder will be the extensions folder with its dictionaries.

The folder with the additional libraries is helpful if you are releasing an international solution. If your solution is limited to one geographic area or one language group, then you can safely delete all of the extra dictionaries. This will save you many megabytes of additional space and reduce your file size, making it easier for people to download when they purchase or demo it.

Keeping it all together

Keep all of the runtime files together. You will need them all to make your product work. You can compress these files in a .zip format and upload them to your commerce site (which we will talk about later).

Selling Runtimes

Selling stand alone applications

Now that you have created your FileMaker product, and released it in runtime mode, it is time to start selling it!

One discussion point worth considering is how do you even explain the difference between a runtime and the typical FileMaker Client-Server model to your target audience?

Nick Orr of Goya, Australia, had some good advice on this:

"For other products, your end user won't know and won't care about the difference and so you shouldn't even mention it to them. Instead you should be talking about a single user version vs a multi-user version. Keep the language suited to the audience and hide the complexity wherever possible."

Perhaps you have a couple versions of your product available, one as a runtime, and one as a networkable standard FileMaker product. From your customers perspective, as Nick has said you would just ask them if they want a single user or a multi-user version. Make it easy for your customer to decide on the version they want to buy.

Problems with deployment to individuals (not using Server):

When you deploy a runtime to people by selling individual, stand-alone copies, there are a few issues to be aware of:

1. It is a large undertaking to support hundreds of individual apps on individual machines.

2. It is a challenge to support both Windows and Mac versions of the same runtime software.

3. Licensing is harder to track

Create a runtime installer

Runtimes are best suited to be easily sell-able commercial apps for the general public who may not be technically inclined. Therefore, the solution has to be dead simple. This would include the matter of installation. I've had many Windows customers contact me who couldn't figure out how to unzip their files.

They will need help with installation of your product, so you will need a good installer. I've tried several different installers to make it easy for my customers, especially the

Windows users, to unpack and install the runtime on their system.

So what installers should you use?

There are several installers out there which will do the trick for you.

In a conversation with Cindy Zelinske, Databug, Chicago, who makes and sells FileMaker products, she said:

"I create the runtime, and use "SetUp Factory" by Indigo Rose for a couple of hundred dollars. I use it to set up the install files, bring in the runtime, create folders and include documentation and videos, and zips it so it is one exe. file and walks them through it, and puts icon on the desktop."

For myself, I use Actual Installer, which provides desktop shortcuts for PC users.

Conclusion

Runtimes are a great option for many FileMaker products. Examine your industry, and work through the decision points in this book to help you decide if it's right for you.

Chapter Seven - Special Focus: Mobile Products

If you are going to release a killer product you must plan for and release a mobile version.

FileMaker GO 13

FileMaker Go was a game changer ever since its introduction. Go11 was pricey, but Go12 changed things because it was free. Go 13 is even better. Here's why:

Benefits of Go13:
1. Go 13 has a cleaner interface with its new home screen.
2. Scrolling is smoother.
3. Script trigger - OnLayoutSizeChange - This new function provides feedback when rotating a mobile device.
4. Improved bar code capabilities.
5. Improved gesture support with the addition of a left-to-right, two-finger swipe. You now have the option to do a two-finger swipe, left to right on your FileMaker solution
6. Best of all its FREE on the APP store!

The Selling Power of Go Apps

Here's an example of the power of promoting your capacity to create a Go app for clients.

Mike Larkin of MacMagic in Minneapolis, MN was on vacation in Montana, at a fly-fishing store, and they were still using a paper-based invoice system. He told the owner that he could make a POS for him using a website and FileMaker Go. The owner said he was interested in selling all 4,000 SKU's via the website. Mike created a quick website on his server (while still on vacation in Montana), so they could test it out with GO. The owner loved it, and Mike made a sale. Vacation paid for! All because of the power of FileMaker Go.

Size is an issue for mobile

One factor you must consider when releasing a mobile app is size. If you are providing access to data from FileMaker Server, then develop a thin client app and place all data on the server. Just use GO to access the data. The other option is to release a fat app with all of the data contained within it.

Selling on the App store?

One of the great advantages of designing your app with FM Go is that FileMaker has done all the hard work of getting app approval. Now any apps created with FM Go are automatically approved for sale on the App store.

Three Keys for Mobile Apps

Three Keys for Releasing an App on Mobile

1st - Single Focus

The best mobile apps are singularly focused on solving one problem. Think of the variety of apps for a smart-phone. One app to creates passwords, another one tracks wi-fi hotspots, and others open shopping sites, etc. The app should be easy to use and easy to understand. No need for user manuals and help screens.

2nd - Simplicity

This doesn't mean simple; it means clutter-free, with each screen designed for one purpose. While a developer may be able to get away with a cluttered desktop application (although even that is becoming a thing of the past), this is unacceptable for a mobile app.

First, you don't have the screen real estate. There is simply not enough room to drop your icons, fields, and text everywhere. Second, people don't have the patience for it. Mobile users want to get something specific done without the delay of trying to sort between various options and buttons.

3rd - Synchronization

In many cases, if you are releasing a mobile app that updates data on a server, you will need to give synchronization some consideration. For example, if sales people out on the road are entering data about customers who already exist in the main system, synchronization will be required.

If your mobile app is connected via a server and FileMaker Go, and you can guarantee that your sales people will never, ever be out of cell tower coverage, then you have no worries. But the reality is that this can rarely be guaranteed so in most cases, you will need to consider your synchronization options.

Synchronization options:
1. Downward only
You download the data onto the mobile device before you leave for the day, and never make any changes to it. It is basically a read-only option.

2. Upstream only
In this case the users may go out onto the highways and by-ways and gather data (like census takers), and then bring the data back to the main headquarters and upload the data.

3. Two-way Synchronization
There are a couple of options to consider:
A. Record by Record Sync - Each record on the mobile solution is compared to each record on the server and updates are modified based on some consistent rules, such as "most recent record wins".

B. Field by Field Sync - In this case, for each record which has been modified, your sync solution will check every field on that record to see which has been modified and when.

This is the trickiest option as the application may be receiving data both in its mobile deployment and desktop. You will need to track when and how data is changed. You may want to invest in a commercially available sync solution like GoZync MirrorSync, or SyncDek.

iPhone vs. iPad vs. Both -- Decision Point

Will you be designing your app for just the iPad, the iPhone, or both?

Some apps may work for both types of devices; some are better for one.

There are significant screen differences between an iPad and an iPhone display. You'll need to consider how people will be accessing the data. What may require one screen on an ipad could take three or four screens with the iPhone.

Of course, there are some ways that you can plan for deployment on both devices. For example, the screen resolution of an iPhone will allow for a 200 pixel wide column. On an iPad, you can place 3 of these 200 wide columns side by side.

The point is, that you must make some decisions at the design stage about how you will deploy your application, and adjust your layouts accordingly.

Container fields and file size

If you are using container fields on a mobile app you will need to give serious consideration to how to prevent file size bloat. When storing the actual contents of various container fields (such as files and images) inside of the FileMaker application, the file size will increase dramatically.

If you have a lot of space and don't plan on moving your database, then perhaps this is not a concern to you. But in most cases, it's considered best practice to keep the size of the FileMaker file down, by using external storage. Choose the "store only a reference to the file" option for your container fields so the pics and vids can be stored elsewhere. Of course, when choosing this option for a mobile solution, you are automatically making the decision to host your solution so your access your data.

Android??

If you want to make your mobile app available for Android devices, then you really only have one option: to provide a web app which anyone, including Android users, can access using their browser.

The Purpose of a Mobile Runtime vs. Desktop

Start with "Why?"

Before you develop your app, ask yourself what is the primary benefit which a mobile version of your app will bring to your product? Will people be needing this particular data out in the field? Will it be easier or more difficult to access this data using an iPhone?

The primary purpose of a mobile app is universal accessibility.

The primary downsides to a mobile app are:

1. Limited screen real estate to display data
2. Less functionality than a desktop version
3. Less processing power
4. Restricted printing options
5. Some networking constrictions
6. Synchronization issues

Which types of Apps need Mobile?

However, having said that, when we ask the question of which types of Apps need mobile, many developers will tell you: All of them.

Because Mobile is the future, and Mobile is now, you need to get your apps onto mobile as soon as possible. And FileMaker is right there to help you into the future with powerful mobile apps that function nearly identically to the desktop version.

Some have made the prediction that all apps will eventually be mobile; that there will not be a distinction between mobile and non-mobile. For example, phones have nearly lost the distinction between home and mobile phones. We will live in the generation where cell phones have become ubiquitous. But how will the next generation interact with phones? A phone is a phone. It will be the same, some argue, with applications. The only real difference will be screen size. We'll see.

But in any case, you must give serious consideration to having a mobile version - or maybe only a mobile option - of anything you make.

Product Focus: Camp Software's GoLaunch

Camp Software & Hal Gumbert

Camp Software released a hybrid product which solves a problem with FileMaker Go.

The problem is that, to use an app deployed with FM Go, users must first launch Go, and then choose the app from the Go launch list. A clever product from Hal Gumbert of Camp Software, called "Go Launch" eliminates this intermediary step.

GoLaunch, allows people to bring up a web page on iOS and opens the FMP url, and launches FileMaker and launches your database. If you go back to Safari, and save it to your home page, and it will open. Never have to use GO at all. It builds an HTTP url which redirects to FMP url.

EasyApps

Chapter Eight - Special Focus: Web Products

Introduction

With the release of FM13, this is a great time to be an FileMaker Developer.

FileMaker is a great tool for deploying your product solution to the web.

FileMaker has a couple of options for you to make your product web-accessible.

First, is Custom Web Publishing.

This technology is based on PHP and provides the maximum customization and power to a web-based solution. Because of the versatility and power of PHP, when it is combined with FileMaker ease of use, you have an outstanding opportunity to develop a powerhouse product.

Be aware however, that CWP is not for the faint of heart. Everything which FileMaker is about in terms of ease of use with GUI-based clickable script development, PHP is not. Unless you are already well-versed in PHP, or have a lot of time to learn it, you may need to hire an outside developer to take your product solution to the web using CWP. There are a lot of great developers who can help with that. I would be happy to recommend any to you.

142

But there is another great option from FileMaker: FileMaker's newest technology, just released in FileMaker 13, called "WebDirect". Using WebDirect in FileMaker, you will be able to build absolutely beautiful and stunningly powerful applications with FileMaker for the web. What's more, if you already know FileMaker then you already have all the skills you need to use WebDirect.

FM13 has vastly expanded FileMaker's reach into the world of web deployment. The new WebDirect features of FM13 brings the legendary easy of use, and excellent user experience to the web for all of your clients. With the release of FM13, the previous web-based technology known as Instant Web Publishing is being discontinued.

Now there is no reason to not develop web-based versions of your product. And some developers may choose to create only a web-based version.

Benefits of WebDirect

FM13 features which apply directly to web-based applications are:

1. HTML5 compliant.

2. Rapid deployment from FileMaker to the Web.

3. FileMaker "themes" based on CSS technology.

4. FM13 has a clean & easy to understand interface.

5. HTTP Post option provides more powerful interaction with data.

6. Server-based graphics which speeds up interactions across the web.

7. Popover Objects; now FileMaker solutions have a similar look and feel to web-based technology.

8. Slide Control; functions like a tab control but without tabs. Instead, small buttons at the bottom of an image reveal additional content when clicked, or on an iOS device, when swiped.

9. Desktop and Browser parity.

FileMaker Pro has done a great job of creating nearly identical experiences between the desktop version and the web browser.

10. Two-way Data Exchange

Another awesome feature of Web Direct is that people can 'drag and drop' files right onto a web direct page and have them loaded into the DB.

11. Script Triggers

Also, script triggers are supported on Web Direct.

"Configure for FileMaker WebDirect" menu item

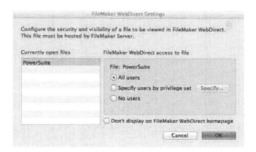

When a file is hosted on FileMaker Server, there are certain settings which need to be in place for people to access your file remotely. This is done through a menu command (File/Sharing/Configure for WebDirect) which provides for security and visibility settings of your application. You must also set the security settings of Extended Privileges to use the 'fmwebdirect' protocol.

Summary

If you are going to be creating and releasing a web-based product, then FM13 is a great option! With the addition of Web Direct technology, you can bring the ease of use and rapid development of the FileMaker platform to your web-based solution.

WorkSheet:
DEVELOPING YOUR FILEMAKER APPLICATION

RUNTIMES:

Will you release as a runtime?

MOBILE:

Will you release your product as a

mobile application?

Does it lend itself to Single-Focus?

Can the interface be kept simple and non-cluttered?

Does it need synchronization? (down, up, both)

Will it be for iPad, iPhone, or both?

WEB:

Will you release it for the web?

EasyApps

Do you want Android users to be able to access it?

SECTION FOUR:
EXTENDING YOUR BUSINESS

Chapter Nine - Starting Your Business

This section is targeted to the aspiring entrepreneurs who not only want to develop a great FileMaker product, but also start their own software company.

The main message which I often heard as I interviewed successful FileMaker companies is that it is one thing to develop a great FileMaker application, but it is quite another to market, sell, and support that product.

For example, consider the legal aspects.

Here are some legal considerations from lawyer, Bill Everett of Buffalo, MN:

Factors to consider when starting a business:

1. LLC

Start a corporate entity, like a Limited Liability Company. Bill recommends that you use the LLC title in all your publications, contracts and correspondence, so that people know they are dealing with an LLC.

2. IP

Intellectual Property Protection, such as registered Trademarks.

Bill Everett says that he likes to pursue a good IP plan, but to do it with a dose of common sense. For example, he asks the question "Who will ever have the money to pay $500/hr to pursue litigation against

149

someone who is infringing your trademark?" So you have to take appropriate steps to protect yourself but realize that if it comes to needing to take someone to court, it is a very expensive proposition. It is much better to be faster and more agile than the copy-cats.

3. Insurance

Get some Commercial General Liability insurance, or Errors & Omissions insurance. He recommends that you buy as much as you can reasonable afford.

4. The Corporate Veil

Be a real business, and keep your business separate from your personal life, in every legal way possible. Treat your work like a business in terms of keeping a true financial/legal separation between your personal home life and the business. This will give you legal and IRS protection.

5. Protect your Users

Make sure that your software is doing enough to protect your Clients data. They will be entering their personal and business information into your software system. Make sure it stays safe.

6. EULA

An "End Users Licensing Agreement" is your protection against unauthorized use or abuse of your software. It also protects you should your software have bugs in it which cause harm to someone else's business.

Your Business Development Universe

So lets put together all of these options now.

If you are creating a product which you will market and sell, then not only will you need to build your product and make sure it works great, but you will also have to build your business development universe. What I mean by that phrase is that you need people to be able to find your product, buy it, and use it.

Everything I am going to share in this section has special application to those who want to begin creating a software company which primarily focuses on selling software as a large part of the business model for their company.

Listed below are the various elements of your business development 'universe'. These all need to be there in some form for you to be successful:

1. e-commerce site

If you are going to be selling software which clients can purchase and use, especially for something like runtimes, or FileMaker Go, then you are going to want to have your own e-commerce site, or rent the use of an e-commerce system. Otherwise, you will only be able to sell software between 9 and 5 or whenever you can answer the phones. That means that the people on the other side of the world from you are out of luck if they want to buy your software. Best to set up an e-commerce option and sell in your sleep.

It is a great feeling to get up in the morning and check the email to see the number of sales which were made the night before while doing other things.

I use 1ShoppingCart.com for my commerce needs. They have all the features such as auto-responders, html and text broadcasts, digital download options (including licensing), upsell features and social media tools. Others have used InfusionSoft, or any of many others. There are a lot of choices out there so do your homework before you commit to one, because it is a major pain if you decide you have to move all of your products somewhere else. Even WordPress has some discount commerce plugins.

2. A Software Installer

If you are going to be releasing an FileMaker runtime, you will need to use a PC installer program. While this may not be as essential for releasing your product on the Mac side, it is absolutely critical for selling and deploying on desktop PC's.

A good installer program will handle the following issues for you:

1. It will put the program in the correct program file directory.

2. It will handle permissions, so that the program will be able to read and write.

3. It will put a shortcut on the desktop.

4. It will put a launch icon in the starter bar

5. It will have an uninstall option.

Do you need a Mac installer?

If you are a Mac user, you know that half the time when you buy a program there is no installer included. You simply receive a splash page with a picture of the software application, and an arrow pointing from the product to the Applications folder. Click and drag and you are done.

So depending upon your particular solution, you will need to decide if a Mac installer is necessary. Some more complex solutions will require an installer. You will need to decide the best option for your solution.

3. A Demo Version

There are a number of ways to approach the issue of Demo versions for your software. Some like to offer a "crippled" version of the software. Even the name tells you that this is a poor choice. Joe King of WorldCloud made some good points about this. Who wants to offer the very first look which a customer takes of your product, and have a number of the key features turned off? First impressions count, and if the first impression of your software is "crippled", so also will be your sales.

Much better to offer a full useable version of the software so that they can experience your software application in all of its glory. You could offer one which is limited to just a certain number of records, or one which has a built in timebomb that turns it off after a certain period of time, typically one month.

In this way, your customers will be able to fully experience your software with all of its great features and benefits. Then when the time comes, you will be much more likely to make a sale.

4. **Authorization Codes**

Every software which is sold has to address the issue of licensing or authorization codes.

The Three "R"s of Licensing are:
1. Registration
2. Randomization
3. Re-use

1) **Registration**

Registration for your product needs to be easy, and it needs to be bullet proof. That is, you don't want to punish customers for buying your product, by making the registration process difficult. (Think Microsoft and their crazy-long authorization codes with no option to cut and paste.) So make it easy, and make sure it works correctly. There is nothing more frustrating in software purchasing than to be told by a registration system that your software authorization code is incorrect, or that your software is pirated, when you know you purchased it legitimately.

Don't make it difficult for your good customers, just because of a few bad customers. Figure out a system that is easy on your customers, and hard on your non-customers.

When someone buys your software and downloads it from the web, they will be using an "unregistered" copy. You, as the software developer, will have to decide what they can do with that piece of software until it is registered.

I have always chosen to allow the software to exist in a full Demo version until registration takes place. This will allow your potential customer to try it before they buy it.

But once they buy it, they will need to register it. What is the best way to do that? What I have done is to allow the customer to purchase an Authorization Code from my commerce site. This way all I am selling when they buy from me and pay the full fee for the software is a PDF. On this PDF is their personal authorization code and instructions for how to register and unlock their software, so that they can continue to use their current software demo.

2) Randomization

Make sure that every customer has to enter a unique code, so that there is no code sharing between friends.

MagicBase Pro Integrated Marketing software does it this way:

When a customer purchased the software, the system was designed to collect some information from them, which was then sent out back to the company headquarters, where they used a proprietary program which I designed for them that would calculate a unique password based on the customers name and some additional data, and then rendered into a different base number system (like Base 11 or Base 16). A certain part of that was then gathered and sent back to the customer. When they entered this number into their desktop version of the software, the application recognized it as a legitimate password, and the system would be unlocked for them.

3) Re-Use

You will have to handle the question of what to do when someone wants to sell or give-away their copy of the software. Will the same code work for someone else, or will they need to get a new one, or even buy a new one?

John Mark Osborn, an excellent FileMaker developer, says that he doesn't even bother with all of this. He does not want to waste time policing people and finding out who paid and who doesn't. So he charges enough up front, and keeps the updates coming to keep and retain his true customers.

Someone else has the system check in once a month, and if the monthly subscription fees have been paid, the system keeps humming along. This is completely transparent to the Customer who doesn't have to worry about re-registration or sending in fees, as long as they are paid up to date the program just keeps working.

Summary

So when you are starting your business there are a few key essentials you need to consider. Take to heart the advice concerning your legal business entity. Then make sure you have the four key elements of your e-commerce business universe of: an e-commerce site, a software installer, a good Demo version, and a good Authorization Code process.

Let's finish up with some excellent words of wisdom from two men who have started strong software companies using FileMaker:

Jeff Duck, Deploy Tech, Florida, makers of Crate Design

Here are some wise words from Jeff Duck of Deploy Tech, Florida. He is an amazing guy who has created the number one product in Crate Design, using FileMaker:

"If you want to really start a business, you need to think long and hard about it.

For people thinking about creating a commercial product for their industry, and wondering if they should shrink wrap and sell it:

*"If you are asking that question, don't do it!"
and "If you are not willing to take it to your grave,
don't start on it!*

*"The product is only the first part; then there is
the documentation, the videos, the installers,and the
business."*

For example, Jeff shares that his product update has
6,000 hours into it. So it is a lot of work releasing a product
and you need to make sure you are up to the challenge."

Todd Geist, of Geist Interactive:

When it comes to using FileMaker to start your
business of selling FileMaker products, Todd Geist explains
why he thinks FileMaker is a great product for productivity
software:

*"FileMaker is the tool that I use because it is
the best between a full programming development
and something that is easier to use. It is the best at
the sweet spot of being rapid and being powerful.*

*Also, it is actually possible for a customer to do
some of their own customization afterwards.*

*A lot of people make the mistake in vertical
markets to ship a product that is completely locked*

down; thus losing your primary advantage of using FileMaker."

~ Todd Geist

Chapter Ten - DeveloPreneur Step #4 - Market Your Product

One comment which I heard at least a dozen times from all of the development companies which I interviewed is that there is a big difference between developing an application for sale, and actually selling it.

When you decide to be a software entrepreneur you are making a decision to take on a whole lot of additional tasks to do besides simply developing an application. In order to begin selling your application, you need to begin marketing it.

Rose Sweeney Rutzen, who is a marketing maven from Chicago, owns her own agency called Loretts Marketing Communication made this statement;

> *"A different skill set and a different personality is needed when you are marketing your product, than when you create your product."*

So get ready to learn a new skill set to sell your product.

You can have the greatest FileMaker app in the world, but if the world doesn't know about it, your business will go belly up. You must learn to market your product. In my interviews for this book, I spoke with several FileMaker developers who said that they nearly starved until they figured out how to market their product.

When it comes to marketing, you need to understand that marketing is a different skill west from development.

Rose Sweeney Lutzen of Lerett marketing Group, in Chicago has said that

"You need to have a unified strategy. And then take that strategy and put it into a work plan."

Craig Motlong, of Pacific Writing says something similar:

"People who work in tech have a different way of thinking than do people in marketing. They are so excited to solve problems from a tech perspective, which is just what you need.

"They build a tool to solve a problem, which is good. But very quickly it grows into something bigger. The products they release have now become their brand.

And you have this responsibility, this expectation from your customers to have more of the same."

Develop Your Story

Craig Motlong says that you have to know your origin story:

"The most successful brands embrace their origin stories and make that a driving force in their brand.

Marketing and branding is about nurturing, growing, and maturing that bond between you and your customers. It is about an emotional connection that happens whether you are trying to do it or not.

Because you are saving them time, aggravation, you are helping them to make money, and see possibilities which they didn't see before. And really good software gives you power, and it excites you, and you get this response: 'It is helping me to succeed ... ' "

Developers need to know this part really well says Dan Miller (no relation), of BizTank:

"There are some core building blocks that need to be addressed.

"1. The Mission of the Company - a long-term goal of the company.
Q: Why do we exist? What is the driving factor that got us started?
The problem we will solve.

"2. Core Values
Once you have the Mission, this leads to your
core values.

"3. Your Vision
A Vision is a "picture of a preferred future."

People jump too quickly to make the product/
software, w/o asking these core issues. If you don't
do this, you will not get the consistency of the
organization, also, trying to solve too many
problems, you hire people with different values and
motivations, or you take on investors who don't
have similar values."

Seven Pieces of the Marketing Puzzle

Marketing Piece #1: You own Website
This is a no-brainer, but how you do it is important.

The Three Things Your Website MUST Do
1.   Add Value
People will not regularly come back unless they find
value on your site.

2. Gather Leads

The real reason for your website is to build your list, so use every opportunity to get a name and an email address.

3. Sell Product

Sell product takes place after you have provided value and gathered names. You don't so much sell your product from your website, as interest people in your product. Then you sell the product using email broadcasts to your list.

One Website per App

The key is to have just one dedicated website per app. I like to use Powweb. They have extremely good rates and a great control panel page with plenty of options for your webpage. At something like $3.80 a month, they are about 25% less than some other well-known sites. I can have four websites, each dedicated to a separate product, for the price of just one website at some other providers.

I have one page dedicated just to SermonBase.

I have another page dedicated to another product I sell to churches.

I have another page dedicated to all of my products assembled into one location.

I have another one for this book.

And I have one for my company.

Website for all Apps

Final bonus marketing option is to gather all of your products into one page (while still maintaining a separate page for each individual product). Does that sound like overkill? Think of it as hooks in the water. The more hooks you have in the water at the same time, the more fish you can catch. If you find an inexpensive web-hosting company and put the sites together with WordPress, you can quickly make very functional and professional-looking websites for not much money.

Use WordPress

WordPress is the best option when you consider the combined needs of being inexpensive, easy to set up, and professional looking.

Once again, if you do not know how to do this, you can hire a great and reliable Virtual Assistant in the Philippines who will put your site up and getting it running for you, for less than $50.

Get a Domains & All Variations

When you purchase a domain for your website, be sure to get the .com domain, and depending upon your focus, .org or .net as well.

And if your product is easy to misspell, then be sure to buy the domains for the misspelled variations of your product name. Then just point those domains towards your main domain, and you are good to go.

Marketing Piece #2:   Website Marketing (SEO and AdWords)

According to Suzie Maier of SM Websites, in MN, you absolutely must have this. It is not optional. I have found in my experience with the five websites which I operate, that when SEO is working well, I tend to get more traffic and more sales. When I don't care to work the SEO, things begin to slide.

Why is SEO important? Because if you are like me, you do not have enough money in your marketing budget to pay for every click you receive.

Here is how Suzie puts it all together:
Suzie Meier:

"1. Bare minimum startup expectations: "To be successful for your on-line piece, have a web presence. Get a WordPress site. Do it yourself or hire someone.

2. GoDaddy has great templates.

3. Set up a Google account: Google Analytics and WebMaster tools.

4. Sign up for local search sites (Google Places)

5. FaceBook page - at a bare minimum."

Marketing Piece #3: Word of Mouth Buzz

Besides SEO, there is a related aspect of this to consider. You need to get people talking about your product. This is not SEO, this is just 'buzz'. Find a way to have people post about your, blog about you, tell their friends about your product, etc. Simple things like discounts or credits to anyone who refers a friend. Or, in the case of free updates for software, here is what I have done. While I charge money for 'upgrades' and do not charge for 'updates' that doesn't mean they are totally free. When I have a free update available, I make it known to my customers that they can get the update for free just by posting a "Like" on FaceBook for my product. This is a cheap and easy way to get some free buzz for your product.

Some marketing ideas:

Idea #1: Related to this, be sure to fill your website with referrals from satisfied customers. I like to sprinkle them all over the website, in the midst of product features and benefits. It makes for a more interesting read.

Idea #2: Here's a great idea: 10% off your next order when you write a review.

This is a great way to spread positive word of mouth about your product.

Benefits:

1. The people writing the Review already like your product, because they want 10% off of their next order.

2. You get content for your website.

3. You set your product up for future sales.

4. They will tell their friends about the great deal.

Idea #3: Make use of some upload sites

Find places where they offer many products for free or demo download and get your product there.

Idea #4: Use Affiliate Marketing

Affiliate marketing means that you get other people to help you sell your product. They take a good cut and promote your product.

Marketing Piece #4: An Ecommerce Ability

Ecommerce - 1SC

If you want an commerce solution, there are a lot of options. I use 1SC and it is used by millions of other people. It is very robust and has plenty of options. Set it up once, and it will work forever. You can always tweak and upgrade as you go. I've hired a Virtual Assistant in the

Philippines who is my product manager and she takes care of all the details.

Here is what you need in an ecommerce solution;
1. A way to sell digital products
2. An Auto-Responder system
   An AR is a way to send out a series of predetermined emails when a prospect signs up for more information about your product.
3. A way to provide Coupons.
4. A broadcast system preferably which allows scheduling.
5. Your own front-facing story that is integrated into your sites look and feel.
6. Good reports.
7. A way to have multiple level user access.
   I use my Virtual Assistant to do many things in the store and trust her. But I retain final access as the store administrator.

Marketing Piece #5: Email Broadcasts

The gold is in the list. You've got to develop your list. There are tons of books out there about this topic. Pick some up. Start developing a list of people who have interests in your product or service. Then once you have the list work it.

When I started, I only did one broadcast a month. That was not enough. So I added another, and now I have expanded it so that I do one broadcast every 10 days. But each one is different. Throughout the month, I do three different types of broadcasts, to appeal to different needs and interests of the readers.

Marketing Piece #6: Blogging

I have found that if I want my list to grow more rapidly, I have to blog on a regular basis. This keeps the hits coming, and grows my list. So put together a good topic list, and a blogging frequency which works for you and then do it. This is called Content Marketing.

An important part of blogging in order to gain notoriety in your application area is content marketing. The goal here is to establish yourself as a thought leader in your industry.

You need to provide real and valuable content to your readers in order to keep them coming back and offer the opportunity to sell them your app. Imagine an app designed for chiropractors to manage their business. You would create a website and blog with advice and help to chiropractors. How to handle customers, how to market, how to run the business, etc.

Marketing Piece #7: Sales Person

This last piece is something which I have not done yet, but I have heard from enough successful companies to know that it is a good plan. Get a sales person to sell your software product. Several companies I spoke with struggled until they hired a salesperson.

Doug Rawson, BaseBuilders, noted that you don't even have to hire a salesperson who is necessarily a techie. They just need to understand the primary benefits of the product, and most importably, they need to know how to sell.

What do you pay your salesperson? Several of the companies just decided to pay their salesperson a straight salary in the early days when sales were slow. A full commission salesperson would have starved. But being able to start with a salary allowed the person to get the sales rolling.

A Sales Person

David Johnson of Facility Wizards has produced some great products, all in FileMaker:
- Asset Performance & Maintenance
- Real Property Administration
- Capital Program and Project Mgmnt
- Enterprise System Integration

He has some great words of advice:
"Advice to Application Sellers:

Lesson #1 - Get a sales person.

Lesson #2 - Get recurring income.

Hired a sales person, and then the sales sky rocketed.

Find a successful sales person; he does not need to be technical; he needs to be good at sales!"

Good advice for you and your new software application company.

But basically, you just have to get out there and sell:

"You inevitably end up doing trade conferences in a vertical market and get a booth, and advertise in the local trade manuals and catalogues. Plus a lot of phone calls."

~ Don Clark, FileMaker Pro Gurus, Albuquerque, NM

Other Marketing Tools:

The Freemium Model

A great marketing tool is to use the freemium model. Give part of your product away, make it useful, but let it create an interest and need for more. Take a look at the App Store. Many of them use the freemium model. Why? Because it works.

Demo's

Providing a Demo copy of your Product is a pretty standard technique. But what kind of a Demo, and how you follow-up on that Demo is key.

Good advice from Joe King WorldCloud about Demo's:

Find a way to let them use it for free. Once they start putting real data into your app, you own them. Find a way to get them in there free first.

Make your Demo awesome! Make it mind-blowing! Put all the best stuff into the Demo. Just make sure that your premium model has even more compelling features.

1. Demo Restriction Options:
   A. Time-Based
   B. Performance-Based

2. What to do when the Demo period is over?

Do you just give a message that time is expired and then shut them down? What kind of options can you give them to move beyond this point, to make their purchase?

3. How to Prevent Demo Hacking

Because a date-based limitation, typically 30 days, is one of the most common limitations imposed on a Demo, therefore BackDating the system clock is one of the most common methods of Demo hacking used out there. This occurs with all kinds of software including some expensive and well-known products by international companies.

How you approach this is a matter of your own particular philosophy. Some people choose to ignore it, feeling that those desperate enough backdate, are not likely to purchase anyway. Others take a more aggressive approach and try to prevent it.

How to prevent system backdating:

1. There is a tool called "ExeShield" which is designed to work with Windows executables and prevent backdating, and many other types of Demo cheats.

2. You could use a free unlock code for your Demo's, which actually has the start-up date within it, but obscured. Then when they register with the free Demo code, the date is included, and every time they start it up, it identifies the date.

But we need to face reality as well. Companies like Microsoft spend millions of dollars every year to prevent fraud and hacking, and they still don't always win. The best course of action for a small company is to stay fast and nimble, and just keep ahead of the fraudsters by providing a great product that people will beg to pay you for, backed up by a constantly changing prevention process.

Finally, Anything Else?

Dan Miller of BizTank has indicated that you need something more to market your product.

"You need a vision and a mission for your product. You must have a greater purpose than simply to make money. You must ask yourself what is your story? What problem are you trying to solve? Why You and Your Product out of the millions of options out there? What is the passion which is driving you to go through all the trouble to make and market your own product?"

The answers to all of these questions are what forms your story. This is the foundation, the baseline, to any marketing which you may want to do.

Summary: Marketing

The best formula which I have found for marketing FileMaker products is the following:

1. Create the product

2. Create a separate stand-alone webpage(s) dedicated just to the product.

3. Make the entire site a squeeze page.
That is, the purpose of the website is to do just one thing: get people to give you their email address, or buy your product. There should be no other distractions whatsoever on the page; save that for later. Right now the primary goal is to build your list, or to sell your product.

4. Buy some Google Ads, with key words targeted to your products.

5. Start an eNewsletter for everyone on your list.
Here is some advice from business consultant Ben Larson of LMCI:
"If sales are not happening:
1. Evaluate the product; is it a good product?
2. Re-brand the product.
3. Get a sales force."

EasyApps

Chapter Eleven - DeveloPreneur Step #5 - Support Your Product

Service & Support, in my opinion, is what separates the mediocre from the truly great companies. Service & Support is not an expense; it is a way of adding value to your Product. Most companies consider Support to be only a money-drain, but if it is done right, it can make you money. In a high tech industry, you must have high-touch Service.

When people think of your product, they think of everything associated with your product, including the service & support. So build a great company image by doing it right. Here's how:

There are the seven benefits of service, all in a handy acronym for you to remember:

SERVICE :
1. Satisfaction
2. Engagement
3. Revenue
4. Value
5. Insight
6. Customers
7. Excellence

1. Satisfaction

If you want satisfied customers, you need to provide them with good quality support and service when they need it. If you take care of them, they will take care of you. If they are satisfied, they will tell someone about you. But if they are *dissatisfied,* they will tell even more people. And that is not the kind of word of mouth advertising you want!

2. Engagement

Customer engagement is a key factor to business success. You need to be able to interact with your customers; get to know them; find out what they like and dislike; find out their needs and values, and in this way, discover other potential revenue streams. In the course of interacting with your customers about your product, you gain all kinds of good ideas, not only for your current product, but for possible other products, or marketing methods. One of my very early customers when I became an independent developer made a suggestion to me about a marketing method which I had considered but rejected as not being helpful. Once the customer told me this was their channel of first choice I began to advertise in that same channel. The result was that I have greatly expanded my business through this marketing, and gained several good long-term customers. All because I was engaged and listening to my customer.

3. Revenue

Service and Support, if done correctly, can make you money, and not just cost money. There are two ways it can make you money: First, of course, is repeat business from satisfied customers. If customers like your product, they will keep using it, and will be there for the paid upgrades, the additional modules purchased, etc.

But the second way that Service & Support can make you money is by providing customized paid tech support for speciality needs. I'm not talking here about charging customers for tech support. I hate that when companies do that to me, and I don't want to do it to anybody else. What I am talking about here are the specialty cases, where someone needs some extra help that goes beyond what could be reasonably be expected for a company to do. For example, in several of my software products, customers want to import their previous data into the software when they purchase it. We provide several free ways for them to do this. We have videos on YouTube, we have documentation and instructions, and we provide phone and email support to questions they may have. But sometimes a customer just can't figure it out and they want more help. So in those cases we offer to do the import for them, for a fee. If done right, your customers won't balk at paying for this level of support because they know you are going above and beyond the norm to help them. They will be satisfied, even though they are paying you!

4. Value

The value of your product is not just the software, but everything associated with that product which helps your customers to solve their problems. When you help them solve their problems with your software product, you are increasing the perceived value of your product in their eyes.

5. Insight

This one is really important for you long-term success: Every single time that you hear from a customer about some problem they are having with your product, you are gaining valuable insight into how to improve your product for version 2.0. You will hear about problems to fix, and extra features to include. And you will gain all of this insight without needed to use beta-testers or usability groups. Your customers, who have already given you money, will now bless you again, but not only giving you money, but giving you Insight on how to improve your product. And that is worth gold!

6. Customers

Good Service & Support will give you more customers in the future. If you treat them well, they will treat you well and tell others about it. One satisfied customer will lead to several new customers.

7. Excellence

Everyone wants to produce a great product, but not everyone is willing to pay the price to have a great product. One of the things which you must do to have a great product is provide great customer service and support. Apple produces some of the best products on the market, and they also have fantastic customer support. They have built great customer support into the cost of their products. So when you pay the "Apple Tax", you are not only buying the product, but you are paying for any future service and support you may need.

When you provide great service and support to your customer, all of the above listed benefits accrue to both you and your customers. And the final result comes to you, you have the satisfaction of providing something with excellence. And Excellence will become a hallmark of your company and all of your products. Great Service and Support is worth it. Plan now to surprise and satisfy your customers with great service.

In summary,
Service and Support can:
1. Keep customers happy
2. Make you Money
3. Enhance sustainability/longevity of your product

Support is the Great Differentiator

We have some companies in the FileMaker community with absolutely great support. One of them is Nick Orr of

Goya. There have been times, when I have posted a question on the public forum about one of Goya's products, and within minutes, Nick will personally reply to me with an answer. And many times this is for a product which he has already given away for free, the Base Elements Plugin.

Eight Support Options for your Product

There are a lot of ways to provide support for your product. Here is a list of eight different ways you can support your product:

1. Email Only

Reply same day to requests. Customers are writing you now, because they have a problem right now. So reply to them in a quick and timely fashion. That is what email is for.

2. Phone Support

This could be a premium option if you like, but I provide this for free to my customers, because that is the way I like to be treated.

3. Web Forums & Wiki's

In this scenario, you provide a forum as a part of your website, where customers can interact with and help each other to use your product well. You can get forum software which can be integrated into your website, for free or a small free. It enhances your product support nicely, and provides and ever growing list of of helpful articles and comments about your software product.

4. On-line User Guide

Unlike a forum, which is created by the public, on online User Guide is created by you. It provides a systematic introduction to, and explanation of how to use, your software.

5. PDF Documentation

PDFs are about the closest we get these days to "printed documentation". Some people like to download and read the whole thing off-line. This can also be a selling feature for those customers who really want to check out all of its features before buying. So make this a free download for anyone who wants it, not just customers.

6. ToolTips

These are the little messages that appear when you hover over a button, or a section of your software. It provides a brief explanation of what this button or section does. If you liberally sprinkle these tooltips throughout your solution, you will vastly increase its usability and ease of use for new customers, and for those trying out the demo version.

7. Webinars

A webinar can be live or it can simply be recorded and made available for download for later listening. There are a lot of options out there for webinar software. Do a web search and find something that works for you. But if you do this option, do it well. Put together a good dialogue script. And if you can include others in the webinar who can ask questions or interact with you, it makes the webinar much more interesting.

8. On-site Conferences

If your software product is hugely successful, then you can take the show on the road! Once there are many users in a particular area, you can always schedule an onsite seminar on how to use your product. Current users will show up, but so will potential new customers. So if you do it well, you can make some money in the process.

Tips for Great Support & Happy Customers

Tip #1 - Plan for Support before you release

If you plan this out, you can build many of the support options right into your product. For example, you can have auto-email links for questions built in to your software. FileMaker has great options for that. You can put in links to videos on your YouTube channel with how to videos for your software. Using the Web Viewer technology you can allow your customer to access your videos or on-line documentation without ever leaving the software.

If you plan your support as you build your product, you can go a long ways towards helping your product be easy to use for your customers.

Tip #2 - Build Support into your Business Model

This is an important tip.

There are two ways to do support: People can pay for support on the spot at the moment they need it, or you can build support into the cost of your product. One method will make customers angry, and they other will make them love you. Can you guess which is which?

Have you ever had a problem with a product, and when you contacted Tech Support, the first thing they say is "Credit Card please".

Mike Clements of Bake Smart, in Indianapolis, the makers of an FileMaker-based Bakery App used to have a business model which required support calls to be an additional charge. He said that customers would always get angry about having to pay for support calls. So they changed their model, required a subscription model that would include the cost of any support calls, and everybody is happy, now that the cost of support is built into one monthly fee. By the way, to keep things simple, they also bundle in the cost of the annual FileMaker license into their product cost as well. People would rather pay one fee, than being "nickel and dimed" to death for everything.

Tip #3 - Use the Help Menu

FileMaker includes a "Help" menu as part of their custom menu system. Make use of it. In all of my software, I use the Help menu for links to on-line documentation, videos, and also links to the other software I sell in the same field.

Tip #4 - Think about what you hate

Decide what kind of so-called "Support" options you personally despise, and then make sure you do not use them on your customers.

Tip #5 - When its time to Reimburse

There will be times with every product, when an unhappy customer will ask for their money back. You need to decide ahead of time how you will handle that. I personally always give customers a complete 100% refund. We have all heard the adage that a happy customer will tell three others, but an unhappy customer will tell seven people they don't like your product. I would rather keep my customers happy. If they don't like the product, I just send them the money back.

However, instead of giving a cash refund, you might consider giving a credit for other products or services which you offer.

Tip #6 - Great Tools for Support

If you want to support your Product well and find and eliminate any bugs, both before deployment or afterwards, then you will need to get your hands on a copy of "Inspector Pro" by Vince Mennano of Beezwax. Vince has been with Beezwax for more than 10 years and developed a great product, which initially just started out as a script analyzer and then grew since then.

It is called Inspector Pro, and it takes your DDR and gives you a much more useful reporting mechanism and analysis tool. Inspector Pro lets you search for almost any thing, script, script name, script step, field table, you name it. It will show you all of the dependencies and what is related to what. If you have ever tried to analyze a DDR, you know the limitations of that report. Inspector Pro is an essential tool for the developer. Inspector Pro is released in two deployments, a runtime version or a fully unlocked file.

Chapter Twelve - DeveloPreneur Step #6 - Upgrade Your Product

If you want to keep the money flowing in, long after your customers make that first purchase, then you will need to plan an upgrade path for your product.

Four Critical Elements to a Smooth Upgrade Process:

Upgrade Element #1. A Policy on Updates & Upgrades

Decision Point: Updates vs. Upgrades
Decision Point: Free vs. Paid

General practice has been that updates are minor changes to your software and are usually provided for free. Upgrades however are more major and are generally sold for a fee.

How you approach the topic of updates vs. Upgrades is also impacted by your business model. Many FileMaker companies have said that the simplest business model is a subscription model which includes all fees, updates, upgrades, support calls etc. Many of your customers' businesses just want a simple clean invoice to pay each month.

Some developers have reported that trying to make a distinction for the customer between Updates vs. Upgrades is just too confusing. No matter how much they reach them and clarify for them, in the mind of the customer it is just a new file that needs to be changed in some way.

This is not an issue for people who are using a centralized solution.

Upgrade Element # 2. An Upgrade Path

Before you launch Product 1.0, you need to know how you will get people to Product 2.0, so you will need to have an Upgrade Plan.

Frequency

You will need to keep a good pace with the right balance between (free) Updates (if you do these), and (paid) Upgrades. It needs to be frequently enough to keep your customers engaged and excited about the progress of your software, but not so frequent that it becomes a hassle. You need to pace out your milestones of the key features you wish to add along the way. Once you have your milestones established, then you can set a time schedule of when each of those new features will be added.

Development

FileMaker Developer Perspective: You need to build in the right scripts, fields and functions, so you can help them move their data from old file to new.

Marketing

Software Entrepreneur Perspective: You need to give them a good reason to both stay with your product, and move forward to the next version of your product.

FileMaker Developer:

Update Methodologies

See this post from Nicholaus Orr on goya.com about "FileMaker Update Methodologies"

FileMaker databases have a particular setup where the data and the programming logic is all contained within a single file. This means it's possible, but not simple, to separate the two and make changes to just the programming logic. Even in solutions using a separation model, there will still be times when you need to make programming changes to your data files. There are two options for that : altering a live solution or importing data into a development copy of the solution.

Altering live solutions is possible and you can manage this easily enough to cause minimal downtime. However there is always the risk, even with products like BaseElements that can document a solution for you, that your changes aren't copied exactly.

Importing data can be time consuming for large data sets, but has some distinct advantages :

- *Repeatable - You can run the import as many times as you need on recent backups without interrupting live files. This way you also know in advance exactly how long the process will take and how long any downtime will be.*
- *Testable - Once you've run an import once, you can easily test the real world results, again without interrupting data.*
- *Flexible - You can alter the imports to only include those files you need to change so that import time is minimized.*
- *Modifiable - Completely changing files allows to easily alter data structures and storage, something that is difficult and time consuming to do manually.*
- *Automat-able - The entire process from start to finish can be set to happen automatically, so that no user intervention is required, and no human errors occur.*

Get UUID vs. Standard IDs

In the words of one FileMaker developer "UUID's are a godsend to runtime developers".

One of the trickiest parts of doing an upgrade is to make sure that all the serial numbers get updated. The usual technique is to use the "Set Next Serial Number" function, and then set the Serial Number to 1 or 100 or 1,000 more than the current max. If you do this wrong, your solution will become corrupted.

But UUID's solve this problem.

Decision Point: Do you maintain the old version(s) and the new?

You options are to:
1. Maintain them both.
2. Maintain the old one for a certain period of time.
3. Drop the old one as soon as you offer the upgrade.

Upgrade Element #3. An Upgrade Authorization Process

How you authenticate your upgrade is major issue.

I like the approach taken by several developers:

Make it easy for your legitimate customers to upgrade. Make it dead simple.

There are a few ways to do this:

1. Keep a separate table of legitimate users which the solution accesses.

2. Build a code translator into your solution so that they enter the correct Authorization Code it unlocks it for you.

3. Use Authentication Methodologies

As you design and build your product, you will need to decide in advance how those Customers who upgrade to your new software will authenticate their software for you. You want to separate out those who are using Demo versions from the actual owners who have paid for the software.

A good option is to provide an "Upgrade" menu item which takes them to a web viewer. This FileMaker Web Viewer takes them to your website where you have a screen which details the benefits of your new upgrade. You want to interest both customers and future customers in this upgrade. Then when they select Upgrade from there, you present them with a price based on whether they are using a free version of your software or a paid copy.

Upgrade Element #4. A Financial Incentive to Upgrade

You will need to decide how much customers will pay for Upgrades. Some experimentation would be in order here. The goal is to maximize the percentage of customers who are upgrading, while also making it a financial benefit for your company.

Keep your current customers happy. I prefer to reward my existing customers for being my customers by making it easy and not too expensive to keep upgrading my products.

Company Focus: Nicholaus Orr of Goya Ltd, Australia

Special Interest to FileMaker Developers:

If you are an FileMaker Developer, then you are going to want to know about Goya, because they can make your life easier.

~~~ COMPANY FOCUS: Goya, Ltd, Australia ~~

What services could you provide to an aspiring FileMaker who is trying to release his/her first product?

Our tools are designed to help developers, and make their life easier. Use BaseElements to build a better solutions, with fewer bugs. Use RefreshFM to quickly build branded updaters that you can send out to users for them to run themselves. And use RESTfm to add a Web Service API onto your products so that your product becomes an integral part of their whole business.

196

For product developers, the big one is RefreshFM because you can build a branded, customised updater in around 10 minutes. If you've ever spent hours or days building, tweaking or maintaining your own update processes, or if you don't even have an automated updater, this thing thing will save you time, money and hair. :)

FileMaker Developer: How to Do One Click Upgrades

My concern as a FileMaker product developer is how I can sell my products to my customers and update them when necessary. My preference is a 'one-click upgrade'.

In this process, when it is time to upgrade, the user opens the new application, clicks on the "Update/Upgrade" button. Then they are asked just one question by your FileMaker application: "Where is the old solution?" Then a file browser pops up, and they select the folder containing their old version of the application.

From that point FileMaker takes over, and exports all of the old data from the old solution, and imports it into the new. Done.

One-click upgrade is a delight to use for the customers.

However, you as the FileMaker developer has to do a lot of work behind the scenes.

FileMaker Developer Process for One-Click Upgrades

If you have a centralized solution, where all your customers access your solution then your upgrade process is much simple than those using a distributed solution.

If you have a distributed solution then you will need to use this upgrade technique.

How we did it with MagicBase:

1. Customers downloaded the Demo file. Using a file plugin from Troi, they are instructed to select the folder that contains their original file. Once they do that, the Upgrader takes care of the rest.

2. The upgrade process would install the new file, and then copy all of the old records into the new solution. This can be quite complex, sometimes requiring multiple recursive loops to track the data.

3. We would provide an upgrade splash screen that would detail progress of the upgrade. By using a series of merge variables, and regular screen refreshes, we would present a scrolling list of actions happening behind the scenes with their software. This would make it interesting for the customer and let them know that yes, the upgrade is still happening and the software didn't just 'hang' but is doing work behind the scenes.

Upgrade Method:

Upgrade Method Steps for FileMaker Software:

Step #1 - Before you release 1.0, plan for the upgrade
There may be scripts you need to build into version 1.0 which will allow you to upgrade to 2.0

Step #2 - Prepare your Filenames and Folders for Upgrades
1. Use a file naming convention that you build into the Import scripts
2. Use a standard folder location where they can be found. I like to call the folder, "EXPORTS", and place it in the root directory of the main file.

Step #3 - Get a File Plugin
Create an 'Import/Upgrade' script which accesses the original file. To do this you will need to use a plugin which accesses files. This could be Troi, BaseElements, ScriptMaster, or whatever. We started with Troi, but found that the Base Elements plugin is easier to use, since no registration of the plugin is required.

Step #4 - Move the File to the new location, so your system knows where it is.

Step #5. Set the import script to import from every table

Go to Layout

Show All Records

Sort Ascending

Go to Last Record

Set Next Serial Number to Max +1

(If you use UUIDs in FileMaker, then Step #5 is unnecessary.)

Plug ins to locate folders & fields

Great Plugins for this:

1. Scriptmaster   Free
2. Base Elements   Free

ReadMe file

I like to list a a history of progress for the upgrades and updates.

What's changed, start up script with a one-time flag

Also in the Startup script for the upgraded file, set a flag which checks if this is the first time the new program is being run. If it is, then show a brief announcement or video showing what has changed.

Options:

1. Put a video in a container field
2. Put a video in a web viewer

3. Just bring up an Announcement layout

4. Download a PDF listing what's new

Upgrade Ideas

Jonathan Fletcher of Fletcher Consulting has some great ideas about upgrades:

Jonathan does not use separation model, so when you upgrade there is an elaborate script. When they get the new version, they click the "Update" buttons which asks where is the last back-up, and then as Jonathan says, "Go have a cup of coffee". It takes 20-60 minutes to update. It updates all S/N's. But now he uses UUIDs for all things. He says, "Especially with syncing needs these days, UUID's are a godsend!"

You can use the same global in a parent table and it will connect and relate to whatever child table is appropriate and activate the correct relationship So one link can connect to different tables!

For Backups, Jonathan does a 'save a copy' script with a TimeStamp, and then creates a backup folder and stores the backup file, using Troi File Plugin. He also creates a menu key combo to save a backup whenever the client wants.

Also when doing upgrades, you can check for the version numbers and when they update, it checks for the version and depending upon which it is, makes different corrections and changes to it.

He also uses a Value List table rather than the Value Lists themselves, because VL's aren't updated with upgrades and imports, so if you want them transferred over they need to be in a table.

Happy Software's Joe Mastrianni does Updates on a twice a year schedule (free) and a paid Upgrade about every 18 months.

Some developers use the data separation model and so an update is simply a matter of swapping out the interface file. In those cases the Update is free. But if they have to make changes to the Data file, then it is more work, becomes an Upgrade and the customer is charged a fee.

Here are some additional Upgrade and Update practices for various developers:

• One developer of a major engineering software provide updates about every two months, which is pretty frequent.
• Another developer charges a flat $49 for every upgrade.
• Another one makes a DIY Update, which is free, as long as the customers do it themselves.
• Doug Rawson, maker of Praesto A/E software finds that customers continue to get Updates and Upgrades mixed up. They even made a comparison of PDF of two columns comparing Update vs. Upgrade and people still don't know it.
• Someone noted that "Windows people don't know how to unzip files; they try to run it from the installer, w/o

extracting it first." So they have to factor that into their upgrade process.

    • Another developer provides a Tutorial Video. They include a link in the Upgrade PDF to show them how to do it.

    • One developer had their version numbers go out to four digits, which they decided was too much (ex. 9.5.2.v2).

    • You can use container files to hold or download updates for Interface File; Data file; Print file and Archive.

    • When upgrading, be sure to do version checking. Remember that not everyone will do every update/upgrade, so your system needs to be smart enough to figure that out.

    • Authentication - you need to plan out when you will authenticate the new file. Do you do it before the Upgrade starts, to save time, or do it after the file is installed?

    • Don't rename fields! This is so you can use the "Matching Names" option on imports.

    • Another developer puts all buttons and graphics in containers, so they can do their own "CSS"; so they can change it in one place and have it all upgraded with a new look.

Summary

You need to ask yourself the question of "Why am I doing Updates & Upgrades?" Is it to develop an additional revenue stream? Is it to delight your customers? To keep up with the competition? This will clarify a lot of the issues related to frequency and costs.

Worksheet: EXTENDING YOUR BUSINESS

Before you go any further, answer the following questions:

1. Do you have the six critical business factors in place?

2. Have you selected an commerce site?

3. Will you use Installer software?

4. Demo - How will you provide Demo versions?

5. Service - Have you decided how to service your product?

6. Support - Which support options will you provide?

7. Upgrades - How ill you upgrade your product?

8. Marketing - Do you have all four critical upgrade elements in place?

9. What is the name of your product?

10. Why did you pick that name?

11. What problem does your product solve?

12. What is the Unique Selling Proposition (USP) of your product? What makes it unique?

13. How will your product make the world a better place to live?

Finally: The Future of FileMaker

The future looks great for FileMaker!

The continued interest in mobile access to data will only continue to grow. FileMaker GO is a great asset for all developers who want to sell mobile access products. This is the number one driving force for interest in FileMaker. Every new iPhone and iPad purchased will create another potential customer who is going to want to access their data on those devices.

The FileMaker WebDirect technology revolution is just beginning! With every new release of FileMaker, WebDirect will continue to improve so that more customers will be able to access their data and interact with it through the web using FileMaker as the backend.

The various design tool improvements in the FileMaker platform have made it easier than every for developers of all abilities to create great looking layouts and appealing interfaces.

This is a great time to be a FileMaker developer and to sell applications made with FileMaker Pro.

_____

If you would like to contact me for any reason, I can be reached at:

Dr. William T. Miller
HighPower Data Solutions
Admin@HighPowerData.com
763-360-4306
Minneapolis, MN USA

Bonus Section:

Companies & Products Featured in this Book

1. HighPower Data Solutions

This is my company based in the Minneapolis metro area. Our focus is on providing customized software for medium-sized businesses who are looking to automate their data processes. We also provide runtime solutions for non-for-profits.

2. Marty Pellicore, Jupiter Creative, Chicago and Jupiter, FL - "Mourning Memories Software"

3. Gerard Beutler, "Pool Pro Software"

PoolPro - track leads, have a job status board; then started marketing it, and building it out from there, adding Presentation Pro which uses content from FileMaker and the sales people use it, service & warranty calls, Perfect Project Pricing (estimating software).

4. Camp Software & Hal Gumbert

- GoLaunch
- ArtLicensing Manager - for artists to track who they have licensed their apps to. They register with their email, and validates against that. It works in PHP and ZoJo.

- Runtime SilentAuction manager, in process, for schools; bar-coding on the bid sheets and the buyers and then links it up;
- They actually sell 9 products, including "FMSB Foundation" starter solution.

5. Nicholaus Orr, Goya, Australia - makers of Base Elements and its plugin

6. Dave Knight, Angel City Data, LA - awesome FileMaker design and development firm - David Knight is a prince of a man who provided great help for this book.

7. Cindy Zelinske, Databug, Chicago. They provide custom DB work. They make Competitive Edge Racing Software. Yes, for improving and winning car races!

8. LifeLab Database Manager, Dr. Bruce Gilbert, NY - seriously detailed software for tracking and managing human tissue for fertility clinics.

9. Geist Interactive
Todd provides advice, consulting, and mentoring to other developers who want to take their products and services to the next level, which Todd calls "meta-consulting".

10. Jeff Duck, Deploy Tech Tech, Florida, CratePro software

11. Chris Moyer, The Moyer Group

12. Ben Larson, LMCI, Delano, MN - Business development consulting

13. Don Clark, FileMaker Gurus, Albuquerque, NM - great blog

14. John Mark Osborn, independent developer well known in the FileMaker community

15. Suzie Meier, SM Website Solutions, Buffalo, MN Services she provides:
- Website Setup
- Full Custom Website development
- SEO Service
- Social Media work
- Blogging - article submissions;

16. Kirk Bowman, Mighty Data, Tyler, TX - value-based consulting and development expert

17. Joe Mastrianni, Happy Software

18. Mark Lemm, LemmTech, San Francisco

Sells "ResourceAce" - data management solution for social service agencies;

19. Marc LaRochelle, Productive Computing, San Diego

- Sells the "Core4" business suite
- "Your AppService" - we make low-cost iPad solutions to introduce people to the iPad solution. This is a $350 template service and layout to get them up and running.
- Provides FileMaker Hosting - because they have multiple data centers across the country, users can get a great experience.

20. Craig Motlong, of Pacific Writing - Business Marketing

21. Joe King, WorldCloud FileMaker Hosting - the best value-priced hosting in the country

22. Rose Sweeney Rutzen, who is a marketing maven from Chicago, owns her own agency called Loretts Marketing Communication

23. Dan Miller, BizTank - business development company

24. Deepali Gokhale, InfoCypher.com

25. Jonathan Fletcher, Fletcher Consulting

26. Steven Blackwell - FileMaker Security Expert

27. Mike Larkin, MacMagic, Minneapolis MN

28. Doug Rawson, Base Builders, makers of "Praesto AE"

29. Vince Mennano, Beezwax, creator of "Inspector Pro"

30. Mike Clements, BakeSmart Software

31. Jason Mundok, FM Developer

32. Paul Costanzo, Madison, WI - "Recruiting Pro"

33. Christian Schwarz of MonkeyBread Software in Germany - great plugin

34. John Sindelar, of Seedcode, in Seattle

35. Matt Petrowsky, FileMaker Magazine - some of the best training in the FM community

36. David Johnson of Facility Wizards

37. Jerry Robin, Transmography, Phoenix - great company name and very witty guy

38. Albert Harum-Alvarez, SmallCo, Florida

39. Patricia Lurvey, of Lyndon Consulting in Chicago
40. Bill Everett, Lawyer from Minneapolis

41. Matt Navarre of MSN Media, in Portland

42. Deb Zempel, of Deborah Zempel Consulting

43. Richard Carlton of RC Consulting

44. Danny Mack of New Millennium Communications in Boulder, CO

45. Court Bowman, ClevelandConsulting.com

46. Jesse Barnum, 360 Works - great plugin

47. David Sanchez, Independent Computer Software Professional - LinkedIn conversation

If there are others whom I have forgotten, my apologies, as the FileMaker community is wonderfully helpful and supportive to anyone who is trying to advance the cause of FileMaker.

If you would like to contact me for any reason, I can be reached at:

William T. Miller
HighPower Data Solutions
admin@HighPowerData.com
763-360-4306
Minneapolis, MN USA

Made in the USA
San Bernardino, CA
28 October 2014